BEING A LOVING WIFE

THE CHRISTIAN READER BOOK ON BEING A LOVING WIFE

Edited by Jeanne Hunt

HARPER & ROW, PUBLISHERS, SAN FRANCISCO
Cambridge, Hagerstown, New York, Philadelphia
London, Mexico City, São Paulo, Sydney

Being a Loving Wife. Copyright © 1983 by The Christian Reader. All rights reserved. Printed in the United States of America. No part of this book may be used or reproduced in any manner whatsoever without written permission except in the case of brief quotations embodied in critical articles and reviews. For information address Harper & Row, Publishers, Inc., 10 East 53rd Street, New York, NY 10022. Published simultaneously in Canada by Fitzhenry & Whiteside, Limited, Toronto.

FIRST EDITION

Library of Congress Cataloging in Publication Data

Main entry under title:

THE CHRISTIAN READER BOOK ON BEING A LOVING WIFE.

   1. Wives—Religious life—Addresses, essays, lectures. 2. Mothers—Religious life—Addresses, essays, lectures. I. Hunt, Jeanne. II. Christian reader. III. Title: Being a loving wife.

BV4527.C53 1983   248.8'43'5   82-48422

ISBN 0-06-061386-6

83 84 85 86 87 10 9 8 7 6 5 4 3 2 1

COPYRIGHT ACKNOWLEDGMENTS

"So You're Going To Be a Bride" by Louise M. Hulst; copyright © 1969 by The Board of Publications, Christian Reformed Church in North America; reprinted from the July 18, 1969 issue of *The Banner* with permission.

"Marriage on the Rock" by Shelba Nivens; reprinted from *Vital Christianity* by permission of Warner Press, Inc., Anderson, Indiana.

"Sensitivity in Marriage" by Robert M. Fine; © 1976 by Light and Life Press; reprinted by permission.

"Called To Be Liberated Women" by Elisabeth Elliot; reprinted by permission of the author.

"Love And Obey—No Other Way" by A. W. Tozer; excerpted from TOZER PULPIT, Volume 5; reprinted by permission of the publisher, Christian Publishers, Inc., Harrisburg, Pa.

"I Prefer Diamonds" by Opal Lincoln Gee; copyright 1968 by *Christianity Today*; reprinted by permission.

"An Undone Marriage" by Dale Evans Rogers; from WOMAN by Dale Evans Rogers; copyright © 1980 by Dale Evans Rogers; published by Fleming H. Revell Company; used by permission of Fleming H. Revell Company and Hodder & Stoughton, Ltd.

"Making Marriage Fun" and "The Difference a Wife Makes" by Robert H. Schuller; from POWER IDEAS FOR A HAPPY FAMILY by Robert H. Schuller; copyright © 1972 by Robert Harold Schuller; published by Fleming H. Revell Company; used by permission.

"Praise Will Get You Somewhere" by Henry Ferguson; reprinted by permission of *The Church Herald*.

"The Couple That Prays—Stays" by Aarlie J. Hull; reprinted by permission of *Herald of Holiness*.

"Must the Marriage Glow End?" by Colleen Evans; from *Decision*; © 1962 by The Billy Graham Evangelistic Association.

"How We Kept Our Marriage Together" by Jeanne Hill; from *The Lookout*; reprinted by permission of the author.

"My Mate—My Friend" by Ed Wheat, M.D.; from LOVE LIFE FOR EVERY MARRIED COUPLE; reprinted by permission of Zondervan Publishing House.

"Whoso Findeth a Wife, Findeth a Good Thing" by Jane Sorenson; reprinted by permission of ETERNITY Magazine; copyright 1969, Evangelical Ministries, Inc., 1716 Spruce Street, Philadelphia, Pennsylvania 19103.

"Have You Loved Your Child Today?" by Rita Carver; from Fall 1979 issue of *Kindred Spirit*; © 1979 by Dallas Theological Seminary; all rights reserved; reprinted by permission.

"Housewife on Holy Ground" by Jane Fader; reprinted from *Vital Christianity* by permission of Warner Press, Inc., Anderson, Indiana.

"Wives: This Is Your Life" by Maryanna W. Johnson; reprinted by permission of ETERNITY Magazine; copyright 1966, Evangelical Ministries, Inc., 1716 Spruce Street, Philadelphia, Pennsylvania 19103.

"One Mother's Choice" by Bonnie Angel; from *Decision*; © 1980 by The Billy Graham Evangelistic Association; reprinted by permission of the author.

"Housewifeitis Is Spreading" by Myrna Grant; reprinted by permission from *Christian Life* magazine, copyright 1964 by Christian Life Missions, 396 E. St. Charles Road, Wheaton, Illinois 60187.

"Faith Tested Our Marriage" by June Williams; from *Home Life*, May 1981; copyright © 1981 by The Sunday School Board of the Southern Baptist Convention; all rights reserved; reprinted by permission.

"What Mothers Are" by Irene Steigerwald; from *Home Life*, May 1968; copyright © 1968 by The Sunday School Board of the Southern Baptist Convention; all rights reserved; reprinted by permission.

"I'm a Career Mother" by Mary L. Sherk; from *Home Life*, October 1979; copyright © 1979 by The Sunday School Board of the Southern Baptist Convention; all rights reserved; used by permission.

"I Married for Love" (anonymous); from *Youth Alive!*; © 1975 by The General Council of the Assemblies of God; reprinted by permission.

"Bringing Up Mother" by Catherine Marshall; copyright *Christian Herald* 1966; used by permission.

"Love, Honor and Obey" by Elisabeth Elliot; from LET ME BE A WOMAN by Elisabeth Elliot; reprinted by permission of the author.

"Is There Love After Marriage?" by John M. Drescher; reprinted by permission of the author.

Interior photographs by Camerique.

Contents

So You're Going to Be a Bride	Louise M. Hulst	9
Marriage on the Rock	Shelba Nivens	12
The Marriage That Grows	Robert M. Fine	16
Called to Be Liberated Women	Elisabeth Elliot Leitch	18
Love and Obey—No Other Way	A. W. Tozer	28
I Prefer Diamonds	Opal Lincoln Gee	31
An Undone Marriage	Dale Evans Rogers	34
Making Marriage Fun	Robert H. Schuller	40
The Difference a Wife Makes	Robert H. Schuller	46
Praise Will Get You Somewhere	Henry Ferguson	52
The Couple That Prays—Stays	Aarlie J. Hull	56
Must the Marriage Glow End?	Colleen Townsend Evans	58
How We Kept Our Marriage Together	Jeanne Hill	64
My Mate—My Friend	Ed Wheat	67
Whoso Findeth a Wife Findeth a Good Thing	Jane Sorenson	74
Have You Loved Your Child Today?	Rita Carver	76
Housewife on Holy Ground	Jane Fader	81
Wives: This is Your Life	Maryanna W. Johnson	84
One Mother's Choice	Bonnie Angel	89
Housewifeitis is Spreading	Myrna Grant	92
Faith Tested Our Marriage	June Williams	96
What Mothers Are	Irene Steigerwald	99
I'm a Career Mother	Mary L. Sherk	101
I Married for Love	Anonymous	105
Bringing Up Mother	Catherine Marshall	108
Love, Honor and *Obey?*	Elisabeth Elliot Leitch	113
Is There Love After Marriage?	John M. Drescher	125

So You're Going to Be a Bride! by Louise M. Hulst

So you are going to be a summer bride! Your letter sounded so happy. I could hear your singing voice and see your sparkling eyes in every word that you wrote. You also sounded very calm and very confident. You are taking "the big step" with very little, if any, hesitation.

I wouldn't shake your confidence. I'm happy that you are so sure that what you are doing is right. Probably this marriage was "made in heaven." Yet I can't resist talking to you as a "Dutch Aunt," sharing with you the thoughts your letter prompted.

You spoke as if you thought marriage was the final step. You wrote of the end of dating, the end of wondering if the one for you would ever come along. It's true that marriage is the end of those things, but it is the beginning of a new part of life. "And they lived happily ever after" may be the conclusion of the romantic stories, but the "I do's" in real life are only the beginning of a whole new life. After the wedding ceremony is over, your real work begins. Then you must face the difficult task of shaping two extremely different people into one solid unit. And this isn't easy. Certainly, God made man and woman to complement one another, and He ordained that they should live together as one. But that doesn't say that it happens automatically with the exchanging of vows and rings. If you doubt that, glance at the divorce statistics. You are both going to have to work at making your marriage a happy one.

Remember the summer trips that you have taken? You planned for months. You saved money, you carefully selected new clothes. All the details of each trip were very carefully thought out and worked out. Yet many couples plunge into a lifetime commitment with little or no planning. Certainly some time should be spent discussing plans for the future and the fundamental principles which will be the foundation of your marriage.

Unquestionably the most important ingredient which goes into the making of a happy marriage is a common commitment to God. This will give your lives the stabilizing influence, the "solid rock" to build upon. God's law and will for your lives will be your guide; where other norms may be relative, God's law is unchangeable. Establish meaningful devotional periods. When differences arise—and they will—you will be able to find unity again in the Word of God.

Right now you probably think there won't be any differences between you. But there will be. Don't idolize him. He isn't a knight in shining armor. He isn't perfect any more than you are. He will have moods, highs and lows, just as you will. He may lose his temper, be sullen, resentful, quiet, just as you may be. So forget your "dream image" now, so you won't be disillusioned when you find his feet of clay. Remember he is going to find out the same things about you.

And when these differences arise, be patient and don't lose your sense of humor. I Corinthians 13, the famous love chapter, talks about knowing in part. This keeps a marriage interesting, but it can also be a trifle maddening. There will be many times when you'll say to yourself, "I just can't understand why he does this or that." But he too will find that you have habits and quirks that he can't understand. So laugh them off. He may like a cold shower while you prefer a scalding hot bath. He may never put his feet on the floor without his slippers, whereas you enjoy padding around barefoot. He may like his toast light and his eggs soft, but you like your toast dark and your eggs hard. He may be astonished at your habit of making faces at yourself in the mirror, and you may wonder why he *has* to put on his left shoe first. But these things won't become issues between you if you keep your smile.

That isn't to say that problems won't come up that can't be laughed off. There will be times when you will quarrel. But establish a few ground rules so these quarrels don't get out of hand, lest you say things to each other that can hardly be forgotten or forgiven. It's good to air your differences. When I hear couples claim that they've been married for a certain length of time and they've never quarreled, I always think they must have all kinds of suppressed feelings which certainly don't go into the making of a healthy, happy marriage relationship. So air your differences, but don't be afraid to say, "I'm sorry," or "I was wrong." This too will help you grow together.

I don't agree with the idea that marriage is a fifty-fifty proposition, or a give-and-take arrangement. An acquaintance once remarked to me, "Yes, our marriage is give-and-take. He gives and I take." I still believe in the biblical principle that the husband is the head of the home. I believe that he should make the major decisions, not in a tyrannical fashion, but responsibly. And you don't have to feel like a martyr when you give in. You will be building a stronger union and a happier home.

Any letter of advice to the "about to be married" has to talk about sex. I don't have to go into the whys and wherefores of the subject. The world, through books, magazines and movies, has taken care of that. But because of these influences, I want to say that I think the wrong emphasis is placed on the role of sex in a happy marriage. I believe that if your personal relationship is a good one, with both showing consideration for one another, the sex relationship will take care of itself. Mere sexual compatibility isn't enough, but if there is true unity in your marriage, sexual compatibility will develop.

So, take this advice for what it is worth. Much more could be written, but I hope this gives you something to think about in the months before your wedding, and after the ceremony is over. Marriage is beautiful, and even though the process of making it such may be difficult, it is worth all the effort. Our marriage form calls a happy marriage a symbol of the relationship between Christ and His Church. Plan together, work together, and pray together for that happy marriage.

Marriage on the Rock by Shelba Shelton Nivens

The other day I overheard a young woman remark about a friend, "I just couldn't stand it if my husband had to go off like hers and leave me for a year or two. They were just so much in love. I don't see how she can go on living each day so calmly and doing all the things that she has to do without him. I know I just couldn't stand it!"

These are the sentiments of many young women who, despite what they know they just could not stand, find that they must stand separation from the men they love while the men fulfill military obligations to our country. And what about these marriages? Will they survive such separations? Very many marriages will not and do not survive separations. So many marriages do not have the right ingredients for survival. There is one very special ingredient in the marriage that neither man, time, nor space can put asunder. I found that this ingredient not only strengthens a marriage so that it can withstand separation but it turns that separation into a very special kind of strength for the marriage and for the individuals involved.

Ken and I were married the day after he completed army basic training. Just the ordinary wedding vows were not enough for two people who had such a special love as we had. In our hotel room after the ceremony, we made our own special vows to God and to each other by reading Jesus' teachings on marriage from the tenth chapter of Mark. God had indeed joined us together. We meant to keep God as the very special ingredient in our marriage that would hold us together.

Eleven days after our marriage, Ken left me to report to ASA headquarters at Fort Devens, Massachusetts, for assignment to a permanent post of duty. It was to be only a short separation. Then I could, I felt sure, make preparations to go with him to his new post. Our God is a kind and merciful God; he would not allow two people so much in love to be separated for very long. But God had long-range plans for our lives that we knew nothing about.

Ken was back with me within the month, but only for another 11 days. After that time he was to report to Fort Lewis, Washington, then to ship out for Japan for two years. That news put quite a damper on my plans to be with him, but only temporarily. Jesus also teaches about faith. Surely, if faith could move mountains and cast them into the seas, faith could move something as small as me across the seas. But even before Ken's ship completed its slow voyage across the Pacific, I knew that I would not be the only one for faith to move across the seas. We were going to have a baby.

It takes a lot of money and red tape to get the wife of an army private to Japan, but I had a lot of faith that I would be there by the time our baby was born. However, God had far greater plans for the exercising of my faith than I. In just a short while, it became evident that I would be having our baby in the States without Ken. That's when I really had to exercise my faith in God—to believe that all things work together for the good of those who love God. When I started wearing shapeless maternity clothes to match my shapeless figure, I really had to exercise my faith in Ken to believe that he was still being true to me, 'way over there among Oriental girls. Lying alone, night after night, feeling the kick of a tiny foot or the beat of a tiny heart just below my own, I could not help but wonder how it could possibly be for our good to be separated at such a time.

I knew without a shadow of a doubt that God had a hand in our lives when he blessed us with the miracle of the life that our love had created. I knew a new closeness to Ken and to God when I first felt in my arms the softness of our new son, Tony, and saw in his tiny features the likeness of his father. While the nurse stood waiting to take him back to the warmth of the nursery, I studied the face in the photograph on my bedside table and then the face inside the warm bundle of blankets in my arms. I clutched my tiny son to me and hid my tears in the folds of his blankets. The nurse took him gently from my arms and left the room with him.

The emptiness in my arms left an ache in my heart. The ache grew stronger as I watched proud new fathers come striding in, all smiles, to their wives' bedsides. Although all the new mothers in the ward were wives of servicemen, I was the only one whose husband was away. "Why," I wondered, "must I be the one to have her child without the comfort of a loving husband? What part could this possibly play in God's plans for our lives?"

I just could not believe that God meant for us to be separated for two whole years. I thought that he might yet perform some great miracle to get my baby and me to Japan. But faith without works is dead, the Scripture says. I went back to work to help finance the miracle I awaited. I found out very quickly that a young woman with a husband overseas is thought of as easy prey for office wolves. And many sympathetic souls were eager to tell me of the escapades of servicemen and their foreign girl friends. But I held tightly to the sacredness of my wedding vows and to my faith in Ken. The knowledge that God was in Ken's life, as well as in my own, made this possible.

Without God in my marriage, I might well have been like one of my girl friends whose husband was also overseas. She did not have this all-important ingredient in her marriage. She believed the tales that she heard about "all" servicemen's amorous adventures overseas. She tried to "get even" with her husband for the things he was "probably" doing. Her marriage was very badly scarred by her actions.

The story of another girl friend's marriage also made me realize that I was very fortunate to have God in my marriage. I had thought her so lucky to be able to go with her husband when the army sent him to Europe about the time Ken was sent to Japan. When Tony was a few months old, they came back to the States full of gay tales of wining, dining, and dancing happily together in Paris. However, a short while later their marriage ended in divorce. They had been able to cut the government red tape that keeps so many couples apart, but even then, their marriage did not survive. It did not have that all-important ingredient.

When I finally faced up to the fact that I would not be going to Japan at all, I accepted it as God's will, but the questions were still there. How could such a separation possibly fit into God's plan for our life together? I could not see then, as I do now, that loneliness and despair caused me to turn more to God to establish a deeper relationship with him. In our longing for each other, Ken and I expressed in letters our thoughts, prayers, and dreams in a way that we might not have done in person. Because we had to stretch our faith in each other and our love for each other across so many miles for such a long period of time, that faith and love were strengthened enough to see us through the many trials that lay ahead in our life together.

    Today, after 15 years of marriage, God is more than ever the one who holds our marriage firmly together, and he makes our love even more beautiful than on the day of our wedding. So, to the young woman who thinks that she just cannot stand being separated from the man she loves, I say, "Yes, your marriage can stand separation—if God is in it. For God is the necessary ingredient for the marriage that neither man, time, nor space can put asunder." ●

The Marriage That Grows by Robert M. Fine

"How could I live with you for 15 years and never know how you felt?" exclaimed a gray-templed attorney to his charming wife in the quiet of my study.

I am continually amazed to discover one element missing in many modern marriages. Within a recent ten-day period a taxi driver in Philadelphia, divorced after 20 years; a young couple in Seattle; and a friend in Los Angeles all agreed: the one quality lacking in their marriage was sensitivity—that responsive awareness of the needs, feelings, and hopes of the other person.

Most marriages pass through three processes. First the marriage is *solemnized* before the altar. In this rite two people become one, hopefully for life.

Then the marriage is *sanctified*. A man and a woman inwardly pledge before God to live together in sanctity.

Finally, every marriage must be progressively *sensitized*. This is the point at which marriages often fail. There is a breakdown of sensitivity. The union degenerates into a tired friendship or a lonely battle.

When married people are insensitive, life becomes burdensome. Like an unsuccessful heart transplant in the body, rejection occurs. No greater instrument of human torture could be devised than a legal marriage binding into one body two people who are each sensitized only to himself and not to each other. Couples bound together in this awful restraint can hurt each other terribly. Because marriage makes us vulnerable to one another, sensitivity without sanctity leads to tragedy; sanctity without sensitivity means misery.

How can we sensitize family life? Paul the apostle said, "Fit in with one another because of your common reverence for Christ" (Eph. 5:21, Phillips).

The sensitivity needed in marriage exists in one body—the living Church which is the body of Christ. "The whole body" Paul described as "joined and knit together . . . and the whole growing up into Christ the living head."

Greater than the wonder of reliability of the senses in the physical body is the mystery of sensitivity within the body of Christ—the Church. This same "mystery" (the New Testament "mystery" means revelation, not concealment) must characterize this most intimate of all human relationships—marriage. "And the two shall become one . . . this is a great mystery" (Eph. 5:31, 32).

I plead for the biblical sensitivity in marriage. Let there be tenderness, sympathy, and self-sacrifice within the body of our marriages like the sensitive love of Christ for his body—the Church.

The Bible urges wives to be as sensitive to their own husbands as they are to Christ (Eph. 5:22–24). How would a woman prepare to meet Christ if he arrived every working day at five-thirty? That imperfect husband at the front door may well stand in place of Christ to the sensitive wife.

Husbands are also to be as sensitive to their wives as Christ is to his Church (Eph. 5:25–32). Remembering that Christ gave himself for his bride, the church, the husband is sensitized to his wife's need for his self-sacrificial love. Reflecting on Christ's future bride—"all glorious, with no stain or wrinkle or anything of the sort but holy and without blemish"—a man is made sensitive to his wife's need for a sanctifying love. If a husband is as responsive to her need for a satisfying love as Christ is to the need of his church, sensitivity will indeed make two to be one.

Called to Be Liberated Women by Elisabeth Elliot Leitch

On a clear, beautiful morning about 15 years ago I was traveling a jungle trail with an Indian named Monga and a woman named Buika. Buika carried a 70-pound load on her back in a basket and a baby in front of her in a barkcloth sling, a package of *chicha* drink in one hand and a machete in the other. Monga carried his blow gun. Period. When we had walked for perhaps three hours, Buika paused to adjust the tumpline across her forehead which bore the weight of the basket on her back. "Why don't you let Monga carry that for a while?" I asked her. She looked at me, startled. Then her face broke into amusement and something like scorn. "Monga? He's a man. He couldn't carry that." Monga's face showed silent assent.

On another occasion in the same part of the jungle, I picked up a barbed spear about eight feet long, lifted it above my shoulder as I had seen the men do, and attempted to aim it. "Everybody get a load of this!" somebody shouted. "A woman with a spear." Sexuality was of enormous importance and interest to the Indians, and although the lines were drawn differently there than in our society, they were drawn boldly and unequivocally.

These incidents provide some clues to the perspective from which I view the subjects of women and liberation. Forced to learn the ways of a people far different from myself, I was forced also to examine my own presuppositions and beliefs. Never again can I regard any issue of universal importance without reference to that segment of my life.

Other things deeply determine my perspective: I am first of all a Christian, which means that everything in this world is viewed with reference to another world. "Faith" is a two-world word, and the working out of that faith in obedience brings me into conflict with ideologies which operate only on the secular level. Ideas such as

"equality," "social justice," and "human rights," regarded in our times as inarguable imperatives, may in the end prove to be pseudo-Christian and provincially Western in their definition. Sometimes we prostrate ourselves before these idols, muttering the required mumbo-jumbo of the sociologists without suspecting that we have perhaps surrendered to secularism.

My perspective is determined not only by having experienced a radically alien culture and by my being a Christian, but by a third factor. I have been, in a very narrow sense, "liberated" in a way I would never have chosen: I am a widow. In fact, I have been single for more than 41 of my 48 years.

I want to talk about a Christian view of women, a Christian view of liberation, and an important distinction which a Christian liberationist must make.

The Nicene Creed begins, "I believe in one God, the Father Almighty, maker of all things visible and invisible." That's where we start. There is an intelligent Creator, a created order, a design. This design includes a hierarchy of beings such as cherubim, seraphim, archangels, angels, men ("a little lower than the angels"), animals, insects, things like paramecia and microbes. Every creature is assigned its proper position in this scale and glorifies God by being what it is. There is no reason to believe that a fox glorifies God less by being a fox than Michael does by being an archangel. I understand that women, by creation, have been given a place within the human level which is ancillary to that of men, and I am glad of this. The Genesis account calls woman a "help, meet"—that is, fit, suitable, for man. I do not hold all men to be so strong, so intelligent, so competent, and so virtuous or holy that they *deserve* a superior position. I simply see that the place is theirs not by merit but by appointment.

The response of the creature to the Creator is obedience, which is a very much more glorious thing in a thinking creature than in a nonthinking one—it is, in fact, a glorious thing called love. And I, as a Christian, can't talk about woman's place or woman's liberation without talking about love.

Each of us, man or woman, ought to recognize his position in the universe. "When I consider thy heavens, the work of thy fingers, the moon and the stars which thou hast ordained, what is man that thou art mindful of him?" wrote the psalmist. The contemplation of all other created things is a great help to the recognition of our own proper significance, and woman's recognition of man, or man's of woman, is profoundly important. We are masculine or feminine by creation. We bear the image of God in one modality or the other, and are affected in our very identity and in the deepest mystery of our being. True masculinity and true femininity, I believe, are qualities that spring from a consciousness of the place and the power granted us by creation. It is a place which cannot be elevated or lowered, or exchanged with any other creature. The power that is ours as women is a power given, not fought for.

The Bible speaks of many different kinds of women. There are slaves, harlots, concubines, wives, mothers, prophetesses, preachers, deaconesses, seamstresses, queens, princesses, shepherdesses, and business women. The woman of Proverbs 31 is represented as a woman of great competence, industry, and managerial proficiency. Deborah was a judge and Esther a member of a heathen king's harem. And of course, at the apex of human history, when the fullness of time was come, a Jewish peasant girl in Nowheresville called Nazareth was selected to do a job no one but a woman could do—Mary became the bearer of the Savior of the world.

Joseph and Gabriel had their part in the great drama, but so far as we know neither protested for equal opportunity. It was Mary's word, "Behold, the handmaid of the Lord," that epitomizes what the attitude should be, not only of all Christian women but of all Christians—a voluntary and joyful acceptance of the responsibilities and privileges laid upon us. For the greatest secret of Christianity, the one hidden for centuries but finally revealed, is that every Christian is allowed to be a God-bearer—"Christ in you."

It is always hard to get at just what we mean by equality. It certainly cannot mean that all human beings are equally intelligent or wealthy or polite or interesting or thin. So equality between men and women is a pretty imprecise, not to say quite meaningless, term. God created man, and God created woman, and has endowed each sex with its peculiar functions and gifts, and within each sex he has allowed diversities of operations, that is, diversities of personality, temperament, ability, intelligence, and shape. We all know some women who are more skilled carpenters or administrators or tire-changers than some men, and we know men who are better dishwashers, or kindergarten teachers, or diaper-changers, than some women. I can't see that there's anything very bad about thinking of women generally as better diaper-changers and men generally as better tire-changers so long as we keep in mind that sex is quite irrelevant to certain jobs. Accepting our places means making it our business first to understand the *cosmic assignment* and then, here and now, to find out what we're good at, and if it is not inimical to God's order, to do it.

Christianity has always given a place of higher honor to women than have the other great religions of the world. Jesus himself honored them, and Paul, that much-maligned and misunderstood apostle, laid the highest demands on husbands when he told them that they must love their wives as Christ loved the church.

To summarize my first point, the Christian believes in a Creator who made everything according to a design. Within his design he set a hierarchy of created beings, each with its given rank. Women are complementary, not competitive, to men. We, too, are allowed to glorify God, and we glorify him by being women. The more womanly we are the more perfectly God is glorified.

Second, a Christian view of liberation. We are fond of quoting, "The truth shall make you free," but the all-important condition is generally omitted. Jesus' actual words were, "If you *continue in my Word*, you are truly my disciples and you will know the truth and the truth will make you free." The foundation is the Word. It is day-by-day adherence to that written Word—what Jesus called continuance—or what we would call discipline that is the price of freedom. It is not bought cheaply. It is not simply picked up here and there. It requires self-discipline and self-denial, and finally—then and only then—it frees. Freedom, according to Christianity, lies always on the far side of discipline. Liberty depends wholly on obedience. And obedience is the fruit of love. "If you love me," Jesus said, "keep my commandments." So we can't talk about liberation unless we talk about love.

What is this "truth" that makes us free? Christianity provides a way of apprehending reality. We understand ourselves in relation to God, to the world he made, to his judgment of what we are (we are "dust, inbreathed with the breath of God"). Our creed outlines this way of looking at things, of apprehending reality. We have said that we believe in a Creator, Maker of all things visible and invisible. God designed things, and we have to know what a thing is for in order to make proper use of it, whether it's a potato peeler or an oboe.

An Auca Indian, for example, discovered that a roll of Kodachrome film fit very nicely into the holes he had in his earlobes. That's making use of a thing, but not the use for which it was intended. The one who makes the oboe knows very well what it's designed for, and it's not up to the oboe to wish for the freedom to be a potato peeler. That would not in any sense constitute freedom. There is a verse in First Corinthians 11 which tells us very plainly that "man was not created for the woman, but the woman for the man."

Freedom is often defined as "doing what you want." One of the first difficulties with this is that few people have any idea what they really want. The next difficulty is that most people imply that doing what they want would entail no restrictions or disciplines. When I've shown pictures of the Auca Indians, who happen to be a naked tribe, people are impressed by their happiness, their simplicity, and what looks like an idyllic "freedom." But the Aucas' survival as jungle Indians is entirely dependent on their rigid obedience to the laws of the jungle. You go hunting, if you are an Auca male, and you make your own blowgun, but you don't make it any old way. You can't decide to be "creative" this time and cure the palmwood any way you please. You can't innovate in choosing the size of the barrel or the design of the darts, and you can't be amiably tolerant in straightening the gun. If you're an Auca female, you make hammocks, and you have to find palm fibers at exactly the right time of the moon, strip them in exactly the right way, wash them and boil them and dry them and twist every inch of some 4,000 feet of fiber in the old, old way to make a single hammock.

The Quechua Indians, another tribe I studied in Ecuador, have learned some new ways from white men. They've decided to do away with some of the old-fashioned laws, and they've begun fishing with dynamite instead of with hooks and spears. They've learned to shoot with rifles instead of with blowguns, and what has happened? They are not free to be jungle Indians because they haven't got any fish left or any game, and they have to learn Spanish and go out of the jungle and get jobs and earn money to buy things the white man tells them they can't get along without, and the first thing they know they're in debt, and what kind of freedom is that? Freedom to live the life of a jungle Indian requires obedience to the rules of being a jungle Indian, and to disregard those rules is to become something else.

I've watched that dazzling dancer Villella leap across the stage—what an image of freedom! He flies. But what an image of discipline and control those beautiful thighs and rippling shoulders convey! I have watched a sailboat racing silently along the horizon—a wonderful thing to see. We say of the dancer, "I'd give anything if I could do that!" meaning, of course, anything but what it takes. We watch the sailboat skimming in the sunlight, but we know it moves only by careful adherence to the laws of wind and wave. A ship tacking against wind and current progresses, but its progress is devious and slow. A ship that is running with a strong tide or a following wind takes to herself the power of water and wind and it becomes her own power. She is liberated, not by breaking the rules but by keeping them. This is what she was made for.

The Christian's true freedom involves a kind of pride. Pride can be a dirty word, but I like the definition Isak Dinesen gives it: "Pride is faith in the idea God had when he made you. A proud man is conscious of the idea and aspires to realize it. He does not strive toward a happiness or comfort which may be irrelevant to God's idea of him. His success is the idea of God, successfully carried through, and he is in love with his destiny. People who have no pride are not aware of any idea of God in the making of them, and sometimes they make you doubt that there has ever been much of an idea, or else it has been lost and who shall find it again?"

This is a very far cry from the sort of pride which says, "We women are as good as you men," and sets out to demonstrate this in a bogus masculinity. This sort of pride is an abomination not only to the Lord but—let's admit it—to most of the rest of us as well.

My acceptance of God's estimate of me is my offering of love. C. S. Lewis wrote, "Wherever the will conferred by the Creator is perfectly offered back in delighted and delighting obedience by the creature, there, most undoubtedly, is heaven, and there the Holy

Ghost proceeds." "Make us masters of ourselves," prayed Sir Alexander Paterson, "that we may be the servants of others." "He that would be greatest among you," Jesus said, "let him be the servant of all."

A Christian's view of liberation is a paradox, contradicting all popular definitions, releasing us to be not just ourselves but something far more than ourselves, enabling us to enter into a fullness of life unimaginable to those who do nothing more than their own thing.

Third, an important distinction which a Christian liberationist must make: as Christians we are at all times to do justice, to love mercy, to walk humbly with God. Those are basic requirements, and have very far-reaching implications for all of us.

In the world, people are generally treated not in their wholeness but according to their function: in business, as brains or hands or customers; in politics, not as persons but as voters. This is legitimate and often necessary, though not always desirable. We ignore sex, color, and creed, and people are more and more coming to be thought of as neuter—sexless, colorless, faithless—in spite of all our talk about treating people as "human beings." As our society increases in automation and complexity, distinctions between people are being blurred, and I for one shrink from it.

My experience of attempting to cross cultural lines in living with Indians taught me the importance of differences. At first I wanted the distinctions between myself and them to fade, but I found that identification is only possible up to a point and is not always desirable even that far. The Indians did not want to see a foreign senora trying to be an Indian, and I learned at last to share the distaste which was instinctive in them. I had to *learn* it because I was from a "civilized" country where democracy and technology had made me lose sight in some measure of the way things are, a country where women, in order to prove that they can do what a man can do, must feel that they must act like men—prop an ankle on a knee, or hold a cigarette between thumb and forefinger.

In the secular world women are nearly interchangeable with men because neither men nor women are treated as whole persons. But the important distinction that Christians make is that women are assigned a *special* place in church and home as opposed to custom in the secular world. In these two domains we return to reality. Women are treated as women, men as men, both sexes as whole persons, divinely created and divinely gifted, all of us complementary members of a single body—a mystical body when we are talking about the church.

As Christ is the head of this mystical body, so the husband is the head of the wife. This is what even Paul calls "a great mystery." It is the earthly image of an eternal spiritual reality, enacted on a day-to-day basis in the home, and continually throughout the universal church. In these two spheres, church and home, in a degree possible nowhere else, the principle of love is in operation. Here we acknowledge gladly our inequalities, we forget about a power struggle or competition or aggression or even so-called "rights," and we accept ourselves and one another for what God has made us, recognizing that, as in a human body, each member contributes to the good of the whole—the hand performing its peculiar function without despising the work of the foot or envying the ability of the eye. One woman may be a corporation lawyer in the world, a devoted wife at home, and a humble communicant at church without violating the design of the Maker. But if in church and home she ignores the revealed design which gives authority to men she is like those people Isak Dinesen writes of who sometimes make you doubt that God had any idea at all in the making of them, or any purpose whatever in the ancient imagery of God as Father, Christ as Bridegroom, and the church as bride, and the relation of men and women as symbols of tremendous heavenly secrets which Christians call reality.

Finally, we women are called, as are men, to discipleship, which means obedience, which springs from love. "Thy will be done," we pray, "on earth"—in my corner of it, in the sphere thou hast appointed me—"thy will be done on earth as it is in heaven." And we can be sure that God is perfectly glorified in heaven. What kind of company there will we be joining? The liturgy of the Syrian Jacobites gives a picture of that gathering which any woman and any man may enter:

"It is meet and right that we should give thanks unto thee, O Holy Trinity. Not indeed that thy majesty requires our praise or has need of our thanksgiving, for those who praise thee are numberless;

clustering cherubim, bright seraphim a countless host, rank upon rank of devouring flame, hidden legions which bear up the chariot of the cherubim, the revolution of whose wheels is infinite; troops of seraphim who by the throb of their wings move the threshold; a shining galaxy which, out of the midst of the burning coal, is discerned by its own movement. Myriads stand before thee, praising thy being, and with one clear voice and one loving harmony cry the one to the other in eternal praise saying, 'Holy, holy, holy.' " ●

Love and Obey— No Other Way by A. W. Tozer

Throughout human existence, the biological positions of the two sexes have remained unchanged but their psychological attitudes and social relations have been altered drastically from time to time.

In recent years there has been a radical revolution with respect to the relationship of the sexes. It is impossible for me to analyze the impetus and the details of this movement which has been widely acclaimed as seeking "liberation" for the world. What I want to say about the relationship of husbands and wives boils down to this: for the Christian of either sex there is only one rule to follow—"What does the Bible say?"

Christians are first of all children of God, and as children of God we are committed to the Word of God. We are committed to a Man and a Book, the Man being the Lord Jesus Christ and the Book, of course, the Holy Scriptures.

In his epistle, Peter makes a plain statement that Christian wives ought to be in subjection to their husbands. This enforces what the Bible seems to teach in other places—that the man as head of the race is head of the home.

Go back to Genesis and you will find that God made Adam from the dust of the ground. Then, because it was not good for him to be alone, God made the woman from a part of the man. But there is absolutely no scriptural authority to allow any husband to behave as a brutal lord or rule his home with an iron hand.

Read again the story of Abraham and Sarah, and you will note the noble leadership of the man Abraham. He never ruled with an iron hand!

Go on to Jacob with all of his domestic difficulties. There was always a graciousness and a kindness within his family circle.

You can continue through Old Testament history, and although it is a bit in the shadows compared with the New Testament, still there was never any brutal masculine domination in the families with whom God was dealing.

In your serious study of the Bible as the Word of God, you will have to agree that it seems to teach that the husband and the wife should supplement one another. In other words, it seems to be the will of God that husband and wife may together become what neither one could be apart.

Certainly the Bible picture is plain in denying the husband any right to be a dominating despot, delighting in hard-handed dealings with his wife and family. But neither is a dominating and rebellious wife ever recognized or approved in the Scriptures!

An overbearing wife is the product of sin and unbelief, and such a role has no place whatsoever in the will of God for the Christian family. I think we may interpret the Scriptures as teaching that God never intended that there should be rivalry and competition between husbands and wives. Rather, it teaches the ideas of understanding and cooperation.

In marriage two people have entered into a covenant by choice, to live in the same home and situation. It should be understood that the husband, according to Scripture and the will of God, is the head of the race and of the home, and also that he should function wisely, according to Peter's admonition: "Ye husbands, dwell with them according to knowledge" (verse 7).

Peter is advising the husband to use the common sense he has been given, "giving honor unto the wife, as unto the weaker vessel, and as being heirs together of the grace of life." Husband and wife are children of God together, equal heirs of the grace of life.

The world in which we live has often sought to satirize the concept of woman as the weaker vessel. But we remember that the Scriptures say the man and the woman are heirs together of the grace of life. Husband and wife, if both are Christians, are united in their strongest bond—one in Jesus Christ their Savior.

Peter makes a strong comment in this passage for the benefit of husbands: "Husbands, dwell with them . . . giving honor unto the wife, as unto the weaker vessel . . . *that your prayers be not hindered.*"

I suppose there are many Christian husbands whose prayers are not being answered, and they can think up lots of reasons why, but the fact is that thoughtless husbands are simply overbearing clods when it comes to consideration of their wives!

If the husband would get himself straightened out in his own mind and spirit and live with his wife according to knowledge and remembering that she is actually his sister in Christ, his prayers would be answered in spite of the devil and all of the other reasons he gives.

There is no place for harsh male rulership in any Christian home. What the Bible calls for is proper and kindly recognition of the true relationships of understanding and love, and a spirit of cooperation between husband and wife.

Peter also gives us a plain answer in this passage concerning the conduct of a Christian wife who has an unbelieving husband.

We must admit that there is the kind of woman who talks about praying for her husband but who refuses the scriptural position of obedience that God has given her. Her husband has never seen any spiritual characteristics in her life that he would want for himself.

Peter could hardly give Christian wives any plainer counsel: "Be in subjection to your own husbands; that, if any obey not the Word, they also may without the Word be won by the conversation of the wives; while they behold your chaste conversation [conduct] coupled with fear" (verses 1–2).

The quiet, cooperative Christian wife is a powerful instrument for good in the home and, without too many words, an evangelist hard to resist. Peter strongly implies that the man, seemingly rejecting her doctrine and laughing at her faith, is badly smitten in his conscience by her meek and quiet spirit and her chaste conversation coupled with godly fear.

We have discussed two extremes—the harsh husband whose prayers are not answered, and the wife whose life does not show consistent godliness. I thank God that in between those two positions there are throngs of Christian couples trying to do the best they can for God in their life situations, living above irritations and together experiencing the grace of God. That is our heritage. ●

I Prefer Diamonds by Opal Lincoln Gee

I'm for marriage! I've read many prophecies that our social mores will change and I have pondered the intensifying propaganda for so-called sexual freedom. Yet I'm still for marriage. I'm for the *freedom of marriage*. The prospect of having a dozen different love affairs during my life appalls me with its *restrictions*—and I say this after being married to the same man for nearly 22 years.

We may as well start with sex. Give me the liberty of the marriage bed. Give me the freedom of a sexual relationship with one lifetime partner. Give me the complete abandon of the physical and spiritual oneness found only in married love.

In marriage there is freedom from fear. How I'd hate to be hemmed in by the fears I know I'd feel in a transitory relationship. Improvements in birth-control methods have taken away much of the fear of conception. Still, thousands of illegitimate babies are born every year. Even in marriage the possible consequence of the mating act can at times inhibit a woman's response to it. Outside marriage, where these fears are multiplied many times, what freedom could a woman enjoy?

There is also freedom from comparison. I am not troubled by a gnawing fear that I might not be living up to a former partner's performance. There is a satisfying security in the knowledge that I did not lure my husband from the embrace of another woman and, because he also wholeheartedly believes in marriage, that no other woman can alienate him from me because her body is more seductive.

There is freedom to grow old within the comfort of my husband's love. I don't think I could bear the agony of being discarded when my physical capacities in this realm, as in others, lose the vigor of youth.

Marriage has made me a mother four times. I would hate to be an unmarried mother, and not only because it is still frowned upon by society. What glorious freedom there is in being able to share the joy of a baby's birth and growth with a husband who feels the same pride and elation in this greatest of all joint enterprises.

There are countless memories of shared joys and sorrows in a good marriage; I'd hate being cheated of these. There have been hundreds of shared small triumphs, and of private jokes that are funny only to us. It takes a while for a man and a woman to build up this kind of easy mental intimacy.

I am not bored but rather comforted by my knowledge of how my husband will react to almost any situation. I don't have to be tormented with self-doubts when he is quieter than usual; years of living with him have taught me that he is worried about something, not disenchanted with me. I wasn't always sure those first few years.

In marriage I find freedom to grow as a whole person. I don't think this would be possible for me with any relationship less intimate and binding. Because I don't have to be constantly concerned with my seduction rating, I have energies with which to pursue my interests and nurture whatever talents I have. No doubt this makes me more interesting to my husband. It certainly fulfills a deep need in me.

I think marriage also enriches my social life. I have more and better friends among both sexes than I could have as a single person. I consider many men my good friends. We have delightful conversations. I don't have to worry about impressing them, and they don't have to be wary of me.

I suppose monogamy is one kind of freedom and the "new morality" is another, and I grant that the price of marital freedom is high. One has to give up a great deal of selfishness in order to achieve peace and happiness with another person. I would not say that my husband and I were each the one perfect choice for the other. At times, we've felt madly incompatible! Yet the territorial rights and freedom of marriage have given us space to grow not only as separate beings but in an ever-deepening oneness that has brought us much happiness.

It has given happiness to four new human beings, too. I can't see how "free love" could ever produce this kind of happiness for people. No doubt, it satisfies physical passion. Yet I wonder how much tenderness you would find in a man unwilling to give his name to and sacrifice himself for his possible unborn child? How much real love is there in a woman concerned only with herself, her sex partner, and the thrill of the moment?

With America's emphasis on sex, it isn't any wonder that young people come to believe that sexual gratification is the "pearl of great price," worth the exchange of all other treasures. Unfortunately, by the time many of them find out that other treasures are highly valuable also, it is too late. They have thrown them away on somebody who doesn't know diamonds from rhinestones.

I believe that the God who made us gave us marriage because he knew it would bring us the highest happiness. Some call this naïveté. Others consider it romanticism. To them I can only offer my own experience in reply: Marriage has brought great happiness to me. ●

An Undone Marriage by Dale Evans Rogers

For years I worried about my background of divorce and remarriage. Every time I picked up the Bible, my eyes seemed to rivet on what Jesus said in Matthew 5:31, 32: "And it was said, 'Whoever divorces his wife, let him give her a certificate of dismissal'; but I say to you that every one who divorces his wife, except for the cause of unchastity, makes her commit adultery; and whoever marries a divorced woman commits adultery."

There it is. Rough. For a divorced person, confronting the Scriptures can be very convicting.

In the Gospel of Mark, the Pharisees were testing Jesus on his view of a man divorcing his wife. Jesus answered them: "What did Moses command you?" And they said, "Moses permitted a man to write a certificate of divorce and send her away." But Jesus said to them, "Because of your hardness of heart he wrote you this commandment. But from the beginning of creation, God made them male and female. For this cause a man shall leave his father and mother, and the two shall become one flesh; consequently they are no longer two, but one flesh. What therefore God has joined together, let no man separate" (Mark 10:3–9).

Jesus didn't sidestep any issue. I am one of those women who was divorced by my first husband, because he wanted to be free of responsibility. I remarried and that marriage also ended in divorce. In 1947, New Year's Eve, I married Roy Rogers, promising God there would never be another divorce in my life, regardless of circumstances. Two months later, I committed my life totally to Jesus Christ, pleading his shed blood for remission of my sins and asking him to take over the reins of my life.

In my experience and opinion, divorce is a taste of hell. No matter who is to blame, it can only be defined as failure to fulfill a contract between two people. In a sense, it is almost like the feeling of losing a part of yourself in death.

I have heard it said that the two most devastating events in life are the sudden death of a child—and divorce. I agree.

In divorce, for whatever the cause, there is a feeling of letting everyone down: your spouse, yourself, and, if you believe in God, letting him down by defying his command: "What therefore God hath joined together, let not man put asunder" (Mark 10:9). I have had that emotion. Divorce, like war, leaves scars.

A few months after I committed my life to Christ, I was reading my Bible one day in the same chapter of Mark 10 which had previously burdened me about my divorce, when another passage leaped out at me to give me hope.

This was the story of the rich young ruler. He came to Jesus and asked what he should do to inherit eternal life. Jesus quoted the Ten Commandments, and the young ruler said he had kept all of them. Jesus must have known the impossibility of that feat, but instead he said, ". . . One thing you lack: go and sell all you possess, and give it to the poor, and you shall have treasure in heaven; and come, follow me" (Mark 10:21).

That was a tall order! The young man didn't like that idea very well because he was very rich. Jesus wasn't commanding money, *per se*, but he wanted to illustrate our inability to reach God or find peace through our own human means.

Jesus looked at his disciples and said: ". . . Children, how hard it is to enter the kingdom of God! It is easier for a camel to go through the eye of a needle than for a rich man to enter the kingdom of God." And they were even more astonished and said to him, "Then who can be saved?" Looking upon them, Jesus said, "With men it is impossible, but not with God; for all things are possible with God" (Mark 10:24–27).

Why should this story of the rich ruler mean so much to me? It made me understand again that the Law stands, but that Christ paid the penalty for our failures. The rich young man was saying, "What should I *do*?" and Jesus said, "Follow me; I will do it all for you." This story comforted my troubled soul.

Don't misunderstand. I'm not trying to climb over the Law of God, or tunnel under it. The penalty of divorce is great, but Jesus can heal the wounds and give us back our health. If we are truly repentant and willing to turn from our wicked ways, he will forgive and heal our hearts, strengthen us with his Holy Spirit, and set our feet in a new, large place of service in his plan for our lives.

Divorce should be the last resort in a failing marriage. The consequences can be so severe.

Look at the children. Torn between the two they love and upon whom they have depended, the children suffer severely. Some say, "It's better for a child to live with only one parent than to live with two who bicker and harbor resentment." If the situation is dire, I agree, but entirely too many people simply get bored in their marriages and look for greener pastures. Often they find the new pastures are not as green and smooth as they first appeared.

Problems in marriage should turn out to be valuable lessons for both parties. You don't quit the classroom because the subject or assignment is difficult. You study the subject to find light for the problem.

Our nation is reeling from the divorce rate. Christians must take a stand on protecting the home, even if it means they are not happy 24 hours a day with their marital situation. Sometimes divorce is the only way out of an unbearable situation, but it is never desirable, because of the trauma suffered by innocent children.

But you say you couldn't possibly forgive him? Look at what he's done to you! He owes you *plenty*! In addition to financial debts, other debts can eat at the heart of a once-healthy marriage. The worst might be the debt of infidelity. "You *owe* me because your infidelity has made me so miserable I can't forget it."

If you are unable to forget, you have not really forgiven the grievance. It appears to me that many men love and respect their wives and yet lie in the arms of other women as if the act had no bearing upon their marriages. I am in no way condoning marital infidelity. There is always penalty for breaking God's Commandments.

Many marriages might be saved—*if* both parties would let go of their pride (which God abhors) and ask for forgiveness and for the grace to forgive each other for whatever indebtedness is felt. There is a certain kind of adhesive that can repair a broken utensil and make it better than it was in the first place. Almighty God has the strongest glue of all, and when he repairs anything it is powerful!

In marital conflicts someone else's pasture looks better than our own. But no field is perfect. Jesus was, is, and always will be the only true perfection. We humans can't realize that our relationships with each other are as strong as our relationship to him in faith—it has taken me many years to discover and experience this truth.

There are many irritations between two people who have committed themselves to each other. When these little things are never resolved, never prayed about, they begin to fester into something that grows into full-scale resentment. Then one day the lid blows off. The best solution is to stop the pot from simmering *before* it begins to boil. Roy and I have made it a practice of trying "never to let the sun go down" on our wrath (*see* Eph. 4:26).

A positive direction is being taken by the church in marriage counseling. The church is the very finest hospital for an ailing marriage. The Body of Christ cares—or should care—about people. Keeping the Bride of Christ healthy until the Second Coming of the Bridegroom should have top priority in God's house.

If a husand and wife would agree with a Christian marriage counselor to help in the healing of their marriage, study God's Word together, pray together, and with the help of the Holy Spirit apply his promises to the problem areas, they would experience a new awareness of the potential for happiness.

What about counseling for divorced and remarried persons? I'm sorry to say that pastors and elders in some churches are unwilling to accept men and women into their membership who have dissolved previous marriages. Jesus, through his atoning sacrifice and the presence of the Holy Spirit in the heart, can build a solid marriage between divorced people. If the parties involved are willing to let God take over, he can and does take questionable material and forge a strong union that unbelievable pressures cannot break. I know.

The Bible says, "Come away by yourselves to a lonely place and rest a while . . ." (Mark 6:31). Jesus knew we must seek solitude at times in our lives. Too often we are so filled with doing that we don't take time to find out where we have been, or where we are going. We women, if we are to be what Adam called us, "Mother of all living" (Gen. 3:20), must do what Jesus said. Periodically we need to withdraw from the hustle and bustle and be refilled ourselves. God will supply, but we must open ourselves to him, quietly, in reverence, anticipation, and gratitude.

After years of public life, I look forward to my long drives across the desert to my plane flights. There I can quiet the tumult of my mind. Just recently one of the news magazines printed a prediction that Roy Rogers and Dale Evans Rogers would divorce this year. This is one of Satan's wiliest tricks. He starts a campaign to provoke controversy about those who proclaim Christ as the answer to life and its problems. Satan loves to see God's children trip and fall.

The prediction about Roy and me pops up about every five years. It causes a little stir and dies a fairly quick death. It is possible that the rumor starts because of my traveling alone. If the rumormongers only knew that the reason our marriage has lasted almost 32 years is because of a mutual faith in Jesus Christ, perhaps they would look elsewhere for such predictions.

I promised God the night I married Roy Rogers that there would never be a divorce, as far as I was concerned, regardless of circumstances. You see, I bear the scars of divorce, and have no stomach for it. However, the most important reason is because Christ has been so real in my life for 31 years, a very present help in trouble, and the Source of my joy in life. Divorce would be an insult to my witness.

I am happier now in my marriage than I have ever been. We have our ups and downs, but over the years have learned to accept and appreciate each other. We enjoy a good sense of humor and can laugh at ourselves.

Commitment is so rewarding. That's true of anything, but especially of marriage. If couples could just "wait it out" in faith and trust in the Lord, there is such a marvelous reward in the companionship of the later years.

One of the problems a man and a woman have is forgetting to be alone together while the children are growing up. Then the children leave home, and the couple doesn't even know how to talk to each other. They have forgotten to be sweethearts in the throes of raising children. I believe this accounts for many of the divorces in midlife. Roy and I were fortunate to be able to travel together in our work. We had time alone together. Our family life was very hectic, with our international family, but God always was the head of our house, then Roy, and then I.

I tried not to interfere when Roy disciplined the children, and he never challenged me, particularly in front of them. There were a few exceptions, but we both tried very hard to have a united front in discipline.

Perhaps you're saying this sounds idyllic, and your circumstances are much different. Women, we may catch perfect moments in our lives, but we are living with problems every day. My friend Carole, who is working with me on this book, refuses to talk about problems, only challenges. It is a challenge to have a marriage that lasts. It is a challenge to live with one person for all the days God has allotted to you on this earth.

We are to love, honor, and obey our husbands as they follow Christ. The Bible says we are to remain with them that they may be won "without a word" (1 Pet. 3:1) by our behavior. That's a tall order, women! We have the natural tendency to want to win them by talking (and maybe even preaching). I do not believe we can ever have that winning behavior if our husbands cannot see Christ in us. On the other hand, I do not believe any person has the right to destroy Christian faith in his mate. This also goes for a believing man married to an unbelieving woman.

When one believes in Christ and the other doesn't, this is one of the most difficult challenges. God is merciful as well as just, and Christ will be our ultimate Judge. Never, never, never give up on Jesus. If you hold on to your faith in him, he will rescue, spiritually resuscitate, and strengthen you to go on, no matter how you have failed.

He rescued me. He can give you his lifeline, too. ●

Making Marriage Fun by Robert H. Schuller

The biggest problem may be to believe—*really* believe—that it is possible to have fun in marriage.

If you plant thistles, you can't expect to harvest grapes. If you plant impossibility thoughts, you can't expect to harvest great possibilities. Launch, then, into Operation Big Switch. That's the exercise of switching your thinking from the negative to the positive. The advice I give here is going to work for you, if you work at it, for I've lived these principles with my wife for over a fifth of a century.

1. *Mind your manners.* The first rule of getting along with anyone is courtesy. It's amazing how we have a natural tendency to be polite when we are in the public eye, while we have an enormous inclination to forget our manners as soon as we close the door of our home and move within a family circle. Common sense should dictate that we would be at our best with those with whom we have continued contact, but such, unfortunately, is rarely the case.

Minding your manners refers to such simple things as cleanliness of body, speech, and dress. It means courtesy, respect, and thoughtfulness. It is a husband continuing to open the door of a car for his wife after they have been married many years. It is a man walking side by side with his wife when they are out shopping, instead of walking three or four paces ahead of her. It is a husband thoughtfully offering to take care of many of the little chores that his wife should not be doing alone.

Of first importance, *find out the sensitive area in your mate's life.* Husbands, find out what about your life bothers your wife the most. Wives, find out what about your life bothers your husband the most.

Chances are you do not realize what about you is most offensive to your mate. I recently played the marriage game with my wife.

I asked her what habit or behavior pattern about my life was most disagreeable to her. I was positive that I knew what her answer would be. I had about three negative factors in my life that I expected her to mention. Instead, she named something that I never thought bothered her at all! We turned the game around and played it the other way, and she had never suspected what qualities in her life I found most potentially disagreeable.

Play the game, then use your head and know that good manners dictate you correct or neutralize this negative quality, promptly and permanently. It may be some little habit, but remember that it's the little things we do and the minor words we say that make or break the beauty of the average passing day.

2. *Never stop courting.* And what is courting but communicating in depth? If there is one major cause of marriage breakdown, it is the breakdown in communications.

This problem is more acute in our day than ever before. We live in a time of telephones, radios, doorbells, special delivery letters, telegrams, daily mail, newspapers and television. With thousands of thoughts bombarding our minds, it is no wonder that we forget to communicate something to our own mate.

So we save one night a week to be alone together. We spend a few hours in an atmosphere where we can open our hearts naturally and honestly to each other. As a result we are in tune with each other emotionally and spiritually. It keeps us living on a close, friendship level.

3. *Manage money or money will manage you.* Know how to handle money and you will eliminate a major cause of marriage problems. If money becomes an end in itself, a distortion of values is bound to create real problems. It is still true that *the best things in life are free.* Since we need money to exist and money can be a great advantage toward improving our lives, it is important that we know how to handle money.

It is very important that husbands and wives should never commit their total earnings to monthly payments unless they have some kind of a reserve for emergencies. A simple technique is easy to remember—when you have earned your money, put 10 percent aside in a savings program of some type. Give another 10 percent to Christ and your church. This does something wonderful: by saving, you are developing self-discipline; by giving regularly to the church, you will be reducing the intensity of selfishness which is the root of arguments and problems. If you can't live on the 80 percent that remains, you are living beyond your means!

4. *Feel free to let yourself go.* Being married in the sight of God and society, release yourself completely in the intimate areas of your marriage. Let no shame, no guilt restrain you from the total enjoyment of marriage.

When God created the human being, he designed us in such a way that we are not complete as a person until we are lost in someone else.

Know that the way to enjoy yourself is never to seek self-satisfaction, but always to seek the satisfaction of someone else. Happiness always comes as a byproduct. Live to bring fulfillment and pleasure to your mate, and you will experience the happy feeling that comes when you see you have brought joy to some wonderful person you love.

5. *Get set for the adventure of discovering new friends.* It's very exciting discovering new friends. Find friends who will be appreciated by both of you. Choose the kind you would like to invite into your home—ones who will unquestionably strengthen your marriage and your love.

We all know that if a teenager gets into the right crowd, he or she can turn out to be a wonderful person. This social principle never changes with the years! A married couple can join the right crowd and things can go great—or they can get into the wrong crowd and mess things up in a hurry.

6. *Establish by-laws on in-laws.* Every corporation must establish by-laws. When you are united in marriage, you are a corporation, so establish by-laws on in-laws.

Some of the things that these by-laws might contain are: (1) No in-law takes priority over my mate. Our love and loyalty to each other are first and foremost. When father and mother give away the bride, it means that the father and mother admit the husband now has first place in their daughter's life. A change of command and a change of priority of influence takes place.

A second by-law for in-laws might be: (2) Never listen to any negative, destructive comment about your mate from your relatives.

Block these thoughts out immediately, or they will become poisonous darts infecting your marriage.

7. *Remember that happiness doesn't come in bottles, boxes, or bags.* Perhaps no problem is more common in marriage than that of problem drinking. Today boxes and bags of narcotics are also coming into the picture.

Again and again the story is unfolded in our marriage counseling. Couples got along fine for many weeks, months, or years, then there was a little social drinking. A husband and another wife had one drink too many, and became flirtatious with each other. When the party broke up, there were feelings of jealousy and hostility between mates. So the beginning of deterioration established itself like an incurable rot in the marriage.

You don't have to become a social drinker in order to be successful, happy, and popular in today's world. It is not uncommon to see a very prominent person refuse to drink in a polite way. Because of the increase of alcoholic problems, the concept of voluntary abstinence from alcohol is spreading across the country today. People are discovering that the safest and the cheapest cure is prevention.

Join the smart set! Be a happy, popular, fun-spreading, nondrinker. Then you can be sure you will never make a drunken fool out of yourself.

8. *Keep on growing closer as the years go by.* Keep no secrets from each other. Honestly share your fears, hopes, and dreams. Never let the sun set on a bad feeling. Talk it out and away before you go to sleep. You must open up, or eventually you will blow up.

There are three kinds of persons. *I-to-I* persons are egocentered personalities who relate only to self-satisfying ideas, offers, and opinions. There is no room for the selfish person in a lasting marriage. *I-to-it* persons are those who derive their main fulfillment from things. Buying, shopping, arranging, admiring, and adoring things is what gives their life meaning. *I-to-you* persons derive emotional fulfillment in relating to people. If you will be an *I-to-you* person, you will grow closer to your mate as the years go by.

In marriage, two persons bring into a union separate sets of values. Each should list them on paper, then rate them in order of importance, until there is agreement. I recommend the following scale. (1) Give God first place. (2) The marriage covenant must come next.

You achieve what you determine under God you *will* achieve. Of course, both mates must agree on this. (3) Children come third. The greatest thing to do for your children is to give them a strong father-mother team!

Give, give in, forgive, and you'll stay close as the years go by.

9. *Keep faith and live happily.* Never break faith with your mate. Break faith, and it may be possible to repair the damage but the scars and cracks will show. Keep faith and you can talk, compromise, cooperate, and overcome almost any problem.

10. *Keep love and you have everything going for you all the time.* Remember that there are three levels of love. (1) I want you, therefore I love you. This is the lowest level; it is hardly more than an animal attraction. (2) I need you, therefore I love you. This is still a very shallow level, often nothing more than lust. It can be noble and worthy, but it is still self-seeking. (3) You need me, therefore I love you. This is love rising to an unselfish level. This is the kind of love that will carry you through almost every storm of life.

The only way that I know for this kind of love to come in and stay in a person's heart is by the Spirit of Christ. We human beings are all born very self-centered and egotistical. The Bible calls this sin. Somehow this self-centered backbone in our spirit has to be broken. This is why Christians speak of conversion—or being born again. Christ can come into a human being and change this attitude fundamentally. You may have plans for a house, a car, a life insurance policy, and a savings account, but unless you have made a personal commitment to Jesus Christ, you do not have the most important thing that you need.

The Holy Spirit in your life is the key that will spell success in marriage. Let him be the head of your home, the unseen guest at every meal, the silent listener to every conversation. Remember that Jesus promised, "Every one then who hears these words of mine and does them will be like a wise man who built his house upon the rock; and the rain fell, and the floods came, and the winds blew and beat upon the house, but it did not fall, because it had been founded on the rock" (Matt. 7:24,25). ●

The Difference a Wife Makes by Robert H. Schuller

Of all the persons in the world, no one is more important than the crowd we call *wives*. "Behind every successful man is a great woman," is a famous and truthful statement. What does every husband want in a wife?

A husband wants someone who fulfills his biological needs, so he seeks a sexual partner.

We must never forget that God is responsible for this thing called sex. God designed and created male and female. "And God saw everything that he had made and beheld it was very good" (Genesis 1:31).

Many counselors agree that sex is a primary cause of problems in marriage. The challenge to wives is to become successful sexual mates to their husbands.

The wife is the happy husband's only "concubine"—consecrated by marriage!

Deep though the biological needs may be, even deeper are man's social needs. He needs one person to whom he can truly open up his heart, his hurt, his hopes. Man wants in a woman someone who can listen to him as he thinks his way through his dreams, and aches his way through his problems.

Marriage, with a commitment to confidential continuity, provides man with a mate to whom he can disclose himself. If he feels assured that this wife is his and his alone for life, then he can trust her with his private, intimate feelings.

What does a man want in a woman? He wants a warm friend, an understanding companion.

A study was made of fifteen hundred marriages, and the number one complaint of men regarding wives was that they talk too much and don't listen enough.

One wife complained to her husband about the bad manners of her new neighbor. "If that woman yawned once, Albert, while I was talking, she yawned a dozen times." To which Albert replied, "Maybe she wasn't yawning, dear, maybe she was trying to say something."

In most adulterous triangles, this is the pattern: wandering husband (or wandering wife)—"I first became attracted to the third party because he (she) was so understanding. It wasn't a physical, sexual thing. It was simply that he (or she) wanted to listen to me and it seemed my wife (husband) never really wanted to listen. It started out as a warm companionship—that's all. Somewhere it got out of hand."

In "Woman's Guide to Better Living 52 Weeks a Year," Dr. John A. Schindler, the counselor, writes wisely: "Love is the combination of sex and deep friendship. The trouble with a lot of love is that it is mostly sex and very little friendship."

Most men might not admit it, but they do expect the women to be the consciences of their lives and their communities.

My wife is my conscience. How I respect her for it! How she helps me! But being the conscience doesn't mean that the wife is to change or convert her husband.

Ruth Graham, wife of Billy Graham, said: "A wife's job is to love her husband, not convert him."

But retain the spirit that can advise, or gently correct. When the wife ceases to be the symbol of The Ideal, all of society will begin to deteriorate. Be a kind conscience!

John Boyle O'Reilly asks in a poem, "What Is the Good?"

> *"What is real good?"*
> *I asked in musing mood.*
> *Order, said the law court;*
> *Knowledge, said the school;*
> *Truth, said the wise man;*
> *Pleasure, said the fool;*
> *Love, said a maiden;*
> *Beauty, said the page;*
> *Freedom, said the dreamer;*
> *Home, said the sage;*

Fame, said the soldier;
Equity, the seer;
Spoke my heart full sadly;
"The answer is not here."
Then within my bosom
Softly this I heard:
"Each heart holds the secret;
Kindness is the word."

What a man wants in a wife is someone who can set the mental climate control to positive thinking. Be a possibility thinking woman.

The wife can be her husband's biggest booster. Wives: nothing is more important than building his male ego. Nothing is more disastrous than neglecting to boost, bolster, and build his ego!

For this reason the most important quality of a successful wife is Possibility Thinking. If a man is dreaming, only to have his wife squelch his dreams and throw cold water on his exciting plans, the marriage is headed for the rocks. No man will ever stop loving a positive thinking wife who feeds his enthusiasm and self-confidence.

How can you be a confidence-generating woman? Listen to Virginia Graham as she wrote in *Good Housekeeping.*

"Everyone needs what I call a Chinese Room to which you can retreat and more or less get reacquainted with yourself. Go in there alone and make a mental market list of what you're doing right, and what you're doing wrong.

"In your Chinese Room, you may come to realize that while you keep your house in perfect running order, and you never forget to put eggs, butter and bacon on your market list, and you never let the flowers wilt in a vase, you may be a lot less careful about how you're running your marriage. A big mirror in your Chinese Room is a must. Take a good look in it. You may see that not only your hair needs a touchup, but your mind does, too. You may feel that you're over-hubbied, but maybe you're really over-hobbied, and hubby hasn't been over-happy for quite a while. Come out of your Chinese Room with the words 'I love you' at the top of your mental market list. Then say the words out loud.

"If your mate seems hard of hearing, it's only probably that he hasn't heard the phrase in so long, he can't immediately recognize it for what it is."

You create a positive mental climate by being a cheerful, happy woman. Pity the man who, tired from a day's work, has to come home to a depressed, fatigued, self-pitying woman. Be proud of your role as a wife and a homemaker. What could be more important!

Catherine Menninger, wife of the famous Dr. William Menninger, relates in a *Reader's Digest* article:

"I remember one night when I lay in bed fretting for hours over my humdrum existence, and envying the exciting, worthwhile lives of the (to me) glamorous nurses who worked with Dr. Will. Sensing that I was awake, my husband asked what was wrong. I burst into tears and began pouring out my frustrations. He listened quietly and then asked, 'Cay, do you really believe that raising our three boys, helping them develop into men with healthy minds and bodies, isn't important work? Nurses can try to cure illness, but you have a chance to prevent it.' "

You create a positive mental climate by being patient. (That's putting off till tomorrow what you'd mess up by doing it today.) Practice the art of tactfulness. (That's changing the subject without changing your mind.) Above all, cultivate the habit of acceptance. (That's loving persons as the imperfect human beings they really are. It's the exercise of mature love.)

Dr. Haim Ginott wrote in *Between Parent and Teenager*:

"Love is not just feeling and passion. Love is a system of attitudes and a series of acts which engender growth and enhance life for both lover and beloved. Romantic love is often blind. It acknowledges the strength but does not see the weakness in the beloved. In contrast, mature love accepts the strength without rejecting the weakness. In mature love, neither boy nor girl tries to exploit or possess the other. Each belongs to himself. Such love gives the freedom to unfold and to become one's best self. Such love is also a commitment to stay in the relationship and attempt to work out difficulties even in times of anger and agony."

To become this kind of person, put God in your life.

A rabbi and a soapmaker went for a walk together. The soapmaker said, "What good is religion? Look at the trouble and the misery in the world after thousands of years of religion. If religion is true, why should this be?"

The rabbi said nothing. They continued walking until he noticed a child playing in the gutter. The child was filthy with mud and grime. The rabbi said, "Look at that child. You say that soap makes people clean. We've had soap for generation after generation, yet look how dirty the youngster is. Of what value is soap? With all the soap in the world that child is still filthy. How effective is soap anyway?"

Religion isn't effective unless used—and it must be used—day after day, after day, after day! Real religious power will come into your life with Christ.

The woman who is alive in Christ sparkles, twinkles, and is a peppy person. She never grows old. Happy wrinkles may come around her eyes, but the eyeballs sparkle with the look of a teenager, into the eighties and nineties!

Jesus Christ knocks at the door of your heart. He says: "Behold, I stand at the door and knock; if anyone hears my voice and opens the door, I will come in . . ." (Rev. 3:20).

Praise Will Get You Somewhere by Henry Ferguson

Last year as my wife and I toured New England we stopped at a farmhouse where a sign proclaimed "Fresh Apple Cider For Sale." An elderly farmer and his wife greeted us. As we sipped cider and talked, the old man remarked that he and his wife had been happily married for nearly 50 years. Then he added, "I reckon the best marriages are really mutual-admiration societies. And it's no good keeping quiet about your feelings. Elsie likes a little compliment from time to time—and so do I."

This bit of rural philosophy brought to mind Oliver Wendell Holmes' description of friendship as "the pleasing game of interchanging praise." Yet how many people praise their spouse after they have maneuvered the family car carefully through a difficult traffic situation? How many praise their spouse when they have remembered to sew on that missing shirt button or perform some mundane household chore?

Shakespeare said, "Our praises are our wages." Since so often praise is the *only* wage a wife or mother receives, surely she should get her measure.

Given such a vehicle for enhancing the self-esteem of others, it is difficult to understand why anyone would not take the trouble to master the art of praising. It is a practice that brings warmth and pleasure into common places and turns the noisy rattle of the world into music. Nowhere is this more true than in marriage. The wife or husband who is alert to saying the heartening thing at the right moment has taken out valuable marriage insurance.

Feelings of inferiority are often the best-kept secret of a marriage that is in trouble and are expressed in many ways. Feeling inadequate is sitting alone in a house during the quiet afternoon hours, wondering why the phone doesn't ring, wondering why you have

no "real" friends. It is wondering why other people have so much more talent and ability than you do. It is feeling unattractive. It is disliking everything about yourself. It is wishing, constantly wishing, you could be someone else.

How can you as a husband or wife help your spouse cope with feelings of low self-esteem? You can make your greatest contribution by keeping the romantic aspect of your marriage alive. Compliment each other. Don't just generalize; be specific. Don't say, "that was a fine meal." Compliment your spouse on a particular dish that was delicious. Don't say, "You look pretty tonight." Point out one thing she has done that enhances her beauty.

If your husband has slimmed down from 210 pounds to 160, don't compliment him by saying, "You look better, dear, now that you're not lugging around all that tonnage." Better to slip your arms around him and say, again, "You sure feel good, now that you're trim again." A biblical proverb assures us: "Pleasant words are like a honeycomb, sweetness to the soul and health to the body" (Prov. 16:24).

Praise is like sunlight to the human spirit; we cannot flower and grow without it. Mark Twain once confessed that he could live for three weeks on a compliment, and he was not an exceptionally vain man. He was just admitting openly what most of us feel privately—that we all need a lift from time to time. Yet, while most of us are only too ready to apply to others the cold wind of criticism, we are somehow reluctant to give our brothers and sisters the warm sunshine of praise.

We don't want to be fraudulent, to flatter, or put into words emotions we don't feel. Such insincerity is easily spotted, and it benefits no one. It is, in fact, a form of cheating. But isn't it cheating, too, when we withhold kind words that a loved one may desperately need to hear?

One characteristic above all others distinguishes marriages that last from those that don't: the willingness of husband and wife to testify in public on each other's behalf. Too often marriage partners will use a gathering of friends as a sounding board to air each other's faults. If husband and wife can depend on one another to testify on each other's behalf—to indicate downright pride in each other—nothing really bad is likely to happen to their union.

Some people seem to have an instinct for sensing the things to say that will bolster their mate's ego. They look at life, so to speak, through their hearts. Lyon Mearson, the author, and Rose, his wife, were married on February 23. "I will never forget our wedding anniversary," remarked Lyon. "It will always be the day after Washington's birthday." "And I will never forget Washington's birthday," his bride answered. "It will always be the day before we were married."

"The greatest efforts of the human race," the 19th century English essayist John Ruskin wrote, "have always been traceable to the love of praise." Nevertheless, most of us in this sophisticated, dehumanized age tend to place checkreins on our emotions. We withhold words of love, admiration, and approval—words that could put the seal of success on our marriages.

Recently a young woman wrote to a marriage counselor. "What's wrong with us?" she asked. "Here we've been married only three years, and already our marriage seems frayed. We both keep trying. Why can't we make it work?"

Later the couple came in for counseling, and it soon became apparent that this was a frayed marriage because the woman was starved for appreciation—as was her husband.

"We both keep trying," the wife had written. But had either ever thanked the other for trying? the counselor asked. Had either ever said, "I know you're making an effort; I need that effort, and I appreciate it and love you for it?" Both admitted they hadn't. As the counselor pointed out to them, this would help fill the vacuum in the soul, this desperate need to be important to someone.

Marriage, we're often told, is a difficult and demanding challenge. It's a relationship in which human beings ask first place in somebody's life. To be needed by someone. And to hear an occasional word of praise from that someone. As the Scriptures remind us, "A word fitly spoken is like apples of gold in a setting of silver" (Prov. 25:11).

The Couple That Prays ... Stays by Aarlie J. Hull

"**M**y husband never talks to me about spiritual things," she said wistfully. "In fact, that night when he was testifying in church was the first I heard about the guy at work he is trying to win to the Lord."

My heart went out to her because I knew just how she felt. I had been there.

From the beginning we have been pleased with our marriage. There have been the usual ups and downs and we've realized that marriage isn't the bed of roses we thought it would be. But all in all, we've been committed to each other and the Lord has helped us a lot.

We had always prayed together, saying grace at every meal; and before we went to bed at night we took turns praying a superficial prayer. But our marriage took a dramatic turn several years ago when we began really praying together. Tim LaHaye, in his book *How To Be Happy Though Married* (Tyndale House), says, "Many a marriage has been completely transformed by initiating a time of regular prayer."

When we began to share our real, deep needs with God in each other's presence, our life together took on new and exciting dimensions.

I soon found that I was the first to know about the things that really mattered to him. I realized and then enjoyed the confidence of knowing that my husband loved me even though he knew my basic weaknesses—that I felt inadequate to face many of life's situations. I rested in the knowledge that he was praying for me.

We shared the indescribable joy and exhilaration of answered prayer. We walked the excitingly adventurous path of faith together—and that made it doubly wonderful. We found that we could lean on each other as we leaned on God.

It was hard at first. I don't know why, but we felt uncomfortable and ill at ease. We had to force ourselves to begin. But once we began, it was glorious, and soon the beginning became easier and easier until it became a part of our life together.

Author-pastor Charlie Shedd and his wife Martha began praying silently together. They would talk a little before prayer about the things that concerned them and then they would hold hands and pray silently. One of them would say, "Amen," and that was that. Gradually they began verbalizing more and more of their prayers until they prayed together out loud. Shedd says that praying together has been for them a transforming experience. Every area of their marriage improved.

Dr. Ralph Byron is chief surgeon at the City of Hope Cancer Hospital in Los Angeles. He and his wife pray "conversationally." This means they pray about one subject at a time. This continues until they alternately have prayed for several things. The burden of one heart becomes the prayer burden of both.

One who practiced conversational prayer in his marriage reported, "My wife and I found that after a few weeks we couldn't always remember who had the burden first, but we came to identify ourselves with each other's burdens. Another blessing we discovered was that in prayer we were reminded to share things that we had forgotten to share because of the busy activities of the day. This sharing further broadened the bond between us."

Time spent together in prayer can become the most valuable time you spend with your spouse. Tim LaHaye summed it up beautifully: "Don't wait until the complexities of life drive you to your knees. If you wait until some difficulty arises to pray together, you will find that when you need God most you know him least. Learn to know him together in prayer now, so that when life's pressure is on you can go in prayer to One you have already learned to know as a close friend.

Must the Marriage Glow End? by Colleen Townsend Evans

When I married Louis, it seemed as if life couldn't get any better. He enrolled in a seminary for three years, and it was an opportunity for me also, because I needed lots of training. After seminary we felt led to go on to more schooling and went overseas to Scotland. I thought, "O God, my cup is so full I don't know what I am going to do."

In Scotland we had a baby. Then I *knew* it just couldn't be any better. It was so good that the next year we had another baby, the next year another. Until now, we have four little stairsteps. We came home and Louis was called to begin a new church in the Los Angeles area.

One morning I woke up and asked, "God, what's wrong?" During the night one baby had awakened and cried. I had nursed him and put him back. A couple of hours later another baby had fallen out of bed, and I had dashed out and put him back. Then the third one—I don't remember what happened, but something did, and I found myself thinking, "The glow is beginning to go."

For the first time I was knowing real responsibility. The hours that I had been able to spend before in Bible study and prayer, I no longer had. How do you find hours for prayer before the children get up? I couldn't beat them at getting up in the morning. It seemed they would even hear me open my Bible. At night, frankly, I was just too exhausted to pray. I was having problems.

So after our first year we took a month's vacation. My husband feels that Christians should be constantly studying, so he went away to study, and we as a family went with him. During that month, I reflected, he could go away and study, but God, You are going to have to give me *my* answer. I don't like these feelings that I am having. I don't like having the glow slip from my life. I feel that victory has gone out the back door.

Here was the first crisis in my Christian life. Each day I would put the children down to nap as fast as I could. I could hardly wait until they were asleep. The moment all was quiet I would get out my Bible and my little notebook and pencil. Then I'd say, "God, where is the problem? Why has the glow disappeared? Where am I wrong? Just show me."

Bit by bit the answers started to unfold. God led me to a certain book which taught me to be honest. It taught me not just to pray about the particular problem that I had myself—"Lord, send me a maid!" No, it told me to get right down to the basics of the problem, which was inside *me*. But the book which was used most of all in my life was the Holy Scripture. I believe very firmly that every single answer to every difficulty in life is there for us.

My first problem concerned my attitude. I felt as if I were a servant in my own home. When the babies cried I would look at my husband lying there sound asleep and say, "Lord, wake *him* up sometimes." I loved him dearly, but he had the most wonderful ability to sleep through everything. Yet I really felt down deep inside that it was my job. I believed that I had been created as a woman, not to glorify myself, but to be a helpmeet for my husband. But when it came right down to the actual test I was chafing and grumbling and resisting and resenting.

My second problem was the physical work—how to get it done. I had been trained to be an actress, not a housewife, and there is a lot of difference. I found that it was hard to get those babies clean and diapered every day and get the house ready for the meeting at night. Our church was started in our home—for four years our home was the church. There were meetings night after night: board meetings, Bible studies, evangelistic meetings for Hebrew Christians in our neighborhood—and cookies to bake for all of them. I found that keeping the house clean, the babies clean, myself clean, left me exhausted. God, how will I get through all this work?

My third problem, as God revealed it to me one night when I became real honest, was what to do about my enemies. Now lots of women I have talked to say, "Well, I'm lucky, I don't have any enemies." I might have said that before that summer. But God showed me that I had many enemies. I was holding certain people at arm's length.

It wasn't that I disliked these people, but perhaps I had heard that they disliked me. Because I knew this, I had put up a little barrier around myself. I hadn't let hate into my heart, but I had let certain exclusive attitudes come into my life. I had simply stayed away from those people. If I was in a room and they were on one side, I'd stay on the other. I just wouldn't get myself close to them.

The next problem I had was one I'm sure you all have had—the problem of interruptions. I found that when we moved into the manse my schedule just had to go. But it bothered me—all the interruptions. I had that ironing to get to, but sure-as-shooting the phone would ring. Not once or twice, but five or six times. And somehow that ironing basket was never empty. Lord, what do I do about interruptions?

The last and biggest problem I had was, what to do about a quiet time? I longed for time with God. I wanted to pray, or I thought I did. I was getting tired of being all Martha and no Mary. Lord, how will I get my quiet time? These were my problems—simple, nothing tremendous, but big enough to eat away the joy of my Christian life.

So I went to the Scriptures, and God revealed his Word to me. The answer he gave for the problem of my attitude of being a servant and grumbling about it was, Christ said, "I came not to be ministered unto, but to minister." In prayer the feeling came to me that I as a wife and mother had the most marvelous opportunity to follow Christ. Christ said, "I came to minister, and the disciple is not above the Master." My whole job in life was to minister, and it had to start in my own home.

I first minister to God by praising him in my home. We can minister to Christ with our love and praise and our public witness, but unless our witness is greatest with our own family, and in our own home, it fails. I found if it doesn't start in my home, I have no right to go outside. I vowed right then that if Louis wasn't the first one to say I was a Christian, I should never again stand up and speak before anyone.

You know, it is absolutely amazing what an attitude can do in the home. If we do things with the wrong attitude I'm sure that our husbands and our families would much rather we would never do them. Only Christ can make us serve with joy and gladness. He is the only one who can change our grumbling into real joy in serving him.

My second problem was work—the plain mechanics of physical work. The verse God gave me for that was the wonderful one, Deuteronomy 33:25, "As thy days, so shall thy strength be." Now I had heard it many times before, but somehow it had never become my own. This time I prayed, "Lord I am desperate. I just have too much work to do."

And in a sudden rush of humiliation I realized that a lot of things in my schedule were not necessary. God had to show me that I was trying to do too much in some areas because of my own ambition. I was taking on too much. But the things that really had to be done, the things that needed to be done, to keep my family happy and well and spiritually whole, I could do—if I would stop worrying about tomorrow. I was always thinking about what I had to do tomorrow. I was dissipating my energy by worry. I realized that I was going to have to stake my life on what God said in that verse. I was going to have to put it to the test.

I have found it true that God always gives us strength for what we must do today if we will let him, and if we will not worry about tomorrow. What a wonderful lesson it was to me to learn to take one day at a time!

Now, what to do about these enemies? How many times have you heard a Christian woman say, "Well I like so-and-so, but she is just not my type. We get along better if we don't see each other."

God made me realize that as long as I had such thoughts I was not following him. It had to be all-out, and he showed me what I had to do. The verse he gave me was from the Sermon on the Mount: "Bless them that curse you, do good to them that hate you, and pray for them which despitefully use you."

I was humbled and humiliated at the thought that I had not followed Christ. God revealed to me that it was a real sin to be sensitive about oneself. So I wrote down the names of these people and started to take his Word literally by praying for them. How wonderful it is to find that some of your "enemies" can become your closest friends.

Now what to do about interruptions. Christ also had interruptions, perhaps more than any of us will ever know—interruptions of a deeper nature. But the way he responded to them is our answer. Do you remember the time when he wanted to be alone with his friends, his disciples, and he said, "We can't be alone here, so let's go across the lake over there where it is quiet; then we will have some time together."

So they pushed off in the boat, and the Scriptures tell us that even before they reached the other side a crowd had gathered and were waiting for Jesus. Some wanted his counsel, some wanted to ask questions, some maybe were curious and just wanted to look. But they had interrupted something that he had planned and wanted to do. Notice how he reacted to it. He simply met the situation as an opportunity rather than an interruption. He talked with them, he healed them, because God put them in his path.

I feel that as Christian women we should treat every phone call, every knock at the door, as an opportunity instead of an interruption. I must admit that it is not always easy, and I mutter to myself as I go to the door. I have to work on myself to keep convinced. But I know that people are more important than my program for the day. I know that talking with someone with a problem is far more important than finishing my ironing. I know that that phone call is someone who has a problem, or maybe just needs to know a phone number, and that even through that I can minister and witness and show love and be a child of the Father.

Now my last and biggest problem was to find a quiet time. How do we, as busy wives and mothers who must put our husbands and our children first, find time to be alone with Christ? All through Scripture God tells us that we need our quiet time, in order to be the kind of people that he wants us to be. I was convinced of this.

The answer that God gave me was mainly an insight into my own condition. I thought I was too busy, but he revealed to me that my problem was not my busyness, but my state of mind. Somehow with all the activities of being a new mother, with a new church and a busy husband, I had allowed Christ to be pushed from the center of my life. In doing that, my burning desire to spend time with him each day had gradually cooled. My busyness was a good excuse, but it wasn't real. The real problem was not my activity, but my affection. When we fall in love, we simply will find time to be with that person; and when we are in the right love relationship with Christ, we will find time to pray.

My mother-in-law was a great help there. She is "tuned in" so that she can go to prayer at the drop of a hat. I am now finding little bits of time all through the day when I can talk to God, if I really want to do it. So this was a most exciting answer. I have learned to pray on the run—on the hoof, as Ruth Graham calls it—in the oddest places and positions; and I have found that God hears those prayers.

It has been a wonderful thing to re-establish a prayer life that comes out of an overflowing experience, one in which you just can't wait to get with him.

I believe that we simply cannot cope with life today without a personal, vital relationship with Christ. And it's so thrilling to see day by day new things unfolding! What a privilege it is to be a Christian, to be a Christian woman, to be a Christian wife, to be a Christian mother. Thank you, God! ●

How We Kept Our Marriage "Together" by Jeanne Hill

My husband Louis and I would certainly have tumbled into the "for-granted" trap had I not been warned about it by a widow who baby-sat our firstborn.

One Saturday I deposited the baby and my sheet of multiple instructions with the widow while Louis waited in the car. Knowing my nature to tarry at the sitter's and repeat my instructions to her, my husband tooted the car horn. When I didn't respond, he gave the horn a heavier hand and I went to the door. "Just a minute!" I shouted angrily. It was then that I heard the widow's voice behind me.

"Young lady," she began, "you're never going to mean as much to anyone else in this world as you do to that man out there in the car."

It was a statement that I couldn't help heeding. For I knew she was right. Louis and I meant too much to each other to treat one another with pettiness.

When I got to the car, my eyes moist at the widow's words, I apologized to Louis. "What's the matter with us?" I said. "Lately I concentrate on every little fault of yours. I used to think of your wonderful side." I kissed his cheek. He admitted the same negative feelings about me. Then we prayed together—something we hadn't done in a long time.

When we got home that evening, we opened the Bible together and read Paul's instructions about marriage. In First Corinthians, Paul says his intention is to "secure your undivided devotion to the Lord," whether one is married or unmarried (7:35, RSV). In order to accomplish that, Louis and I decided to search the Scriptures and to set up a plan to prevent "for-grantedness" in our marriage.

What we came up with has enabled us to sidestep marriage's deadly trap through 25 years of daily living and three children. Here is our plan.

1. *Start your day with a family devotional and end it with Scripture together, followed by prayer.* Many families start the day with devotions, but few follow up with a meditation time with God after retiring to the bedroom.

2. *Give your spouse praise or appreciation every day.* A few thoughtful, honest words of praise can smooth off the rough edges of daily family life. This helps you concentrate on each other's positive points.

3. *Have dinner or dessert out, as a couple, at least once a week.* If possible, have a dinner at a restaurant as a talking time for the two of you. If the budget won't tolerate a meal, make it a dessert that you can linger over.

4. *Take opportunities to see your mate perform in a role outside that of a husband/wife and father/mother.* It will give you a lift to see your mate performing in his area of work or profession. You can appreciate areas outside the home—hobbies, work in organizations, special interests—just as much as a mate's vocation or profession.

5. *When personality clashes occur, hand the problem to God for his solution.* When marriage hangups seem to return through the months, you need to check yourself. Are you *really* handing the whole problem to God, or are you keeping back a few corners here and there? And are you giving him your will in the matter, or are you just asking him "to help" you carry out *your* solution? When both you and your mate are honest in going to God with a plaguing problem, love has already begun the solution inside your hearts by allowing his voice to be heard by you both.

6. *Go on a "honeymoon" once a year.* The reason for a honeymoon is the same as the reason for the first one. It permits the couple's concentrating only on each other.

When you lose wonder from your relationship, you start taking your loved one for granted.

Louis and I have proved these highways to better marriage, and we recommend them to others. ●

My Mate—
My Friend by Ed Wheat, M.D.

"Wilt thou have this woman to be thy wife . . . to live with her and *cherish* her?"

"Wilt thou have this man to be thy husband . . . to live with him and *cherish* him?"

These age-old questions put to the two people saying their marriage vows are always answered: "I will!" But what does it mean to *cherish* a marriage partner, and how is it to be done?

When we understand the love the Greek New Testament calls (in verb form) *phileo*, we will have the answers, and we will better know how to cherish and become cherished in our own marriage.

We find that *phileo* is the love one feels for a cherished friend of either sex. Jesus had this love for a disciple: "One of his disciples whom Jesus loved—whom he esteemed and delighted in . . ." (John 13:23).

Peter expressed his *phileo* love for Jesus: "Lord . . . You know that I love you—that I have a deep, instinctive, personal affection for you, as for a close friend . . ." (John 21:17 AMPLIFIED).

Jonathan and David provide an Old Testament example: ". . . the soul of Jonathan was knit with the soul of David, and Jonathan loved him as his own soul" (1 Sam. 18:1).

God also loves with a *phileo* love: "The Father dearly loves the Son and discloses (shows) to him everything that he himself does" (John 5:20 AMPLIFIED).

The Father loves believers in the same personal way: "For the Father himself tenderly loves you, because you have loved me, and have believed that I came out from the Father" (John 16:27 AMPLIFIED).

From biblical evidence we can make these additional observations concerning *phileo*:

(1) It is emotional in nature and cannot be commanded, but can be developed.

(2) It is a selective love, based on qualities in another person that one finds admirable, attractive, and appealing. (One loves *because* . . .)

(3) It is fellowship-love requiring enjoyable interaction through comradeship and communication.

(4) It is the manifestation of a living, growing relationship between two friends.

This same *phileo* is the cherishing love of marriage. Biblically, older women are commanded to teach younger women how to develop *phileo* love for their husbands: ". . . the older women . . . are to give good counsel and be teachers of what is right and noble, so that they will wisely train the young women . . . to love their husbands . . ." (Tit. 2:3–4 AMPLIFIED).

The fond friendship of *phileo* takes on added intensity and enjoyment as part of the multi-faceted love bond of husband and wife. When two people in marriage share themselves—their lives and all that they are—they develop this love of mutual affection, rapport, and comradeship. They delight in each other's company. They care for each other tenderly. They hold each other dear. This is cherishing!

None of the loves of marriage offers more consistent pleasure than *phileo*. Friendship can reach its zenith in marriage because the other loves of the relationship enhance it. The bond is closer, the setting more secure. The camaraderie of best friends who are also lovers seems twice as exciting and doubly precious.

But *phileo* is by no means a sure thing. It cannot be counted on as a built-in benefit of marriage. It does not automatically appear when the vows are said and the rings exchanged.

In fact, as a counselor, I have observed that *phileo* seems strangely absent from many marriages. Through neglect, couples have lost the rapport they once had. Others never bothered to develop it, perhaps because they did not know how. Or they discounted its importance, leaning more heavily on the romantic and sexual attractions of their relationship.

There is only one way to learn the joy of sharing yourself with another. That is by doing it! *Sharing is the key that unlocks the emotions of phileo love.* This is the fundamental principle to keep in mind as you seek to develop *phileo* to the fullest in your marriage.

Next, consider that *phileo* consists of emotions. Thus, you must establish the right conditions in your relationship to bring the feelings to life. Once evoked, they need to be maintained, again through providing the right conditions.

Remember that *phileo* is the friendship love. The conditions you set up in your marriage must be conducive to friendship. You will need to be sensitive to the basic dynamics determining how friends are made and kept. Of course, these are known by almost everyone through personal experience. It is a matter of applying what you know. Take a creative look at your marriage as a model of friendship—creative because you are seeing the customary in a new way. How can you put the principles that are tried and true to good use in the setting of your own marriage? Picture your partner (potentially, at least) as your best friend. How can you bring this about in fact, applying your general knowledge of friendship to your specific knowledge of your spouse?

Perhaps the saying comes to mind, "To have a friend, you must be one." That is a good place to begin. We have said that *sharing* on all levels is the key. But *togetherness* turns the key in the lock. Consider these three ingredients of friendship and *phileo* love: comradeship, companionship, and communication. Each begins with *com*, the Latin for "together." Comradeship literally means "together in the same chamber or room"; companionship literally means "taking bread together"; communication literally means "possessing together."

Clearly, then, the two of you are going to have to plan for togetherness—the kind that involves mutual understanding and enjoyment. You will have to find ways to share meaningful time. And that is just the beginning. "Being a friend" demands conscious effort and commitment. But becoming best friends with your marriage partner can turn out to be one of the most rewarding projects of your lifetime.

It will be helpful for you to consider what some psychologists believe to be the three phases of friendship, adapted here specifically to marriage. You will see that these involve sharing on successively deeper levels. They can be expected to evolve as your relationship progresses. However, you will never graduate and leave one behind for the next. The accomplishments of each phase belong in your marriage permanently. If you want to remember the phases by name, just think of the little red schoolhouse with its three R's. Friendship has three R's too: relaxation, rapport, and revelation.

Relaxation must take place before closeness develops. It is the time to learn to be comfortable with each other while you practice the basics of friendship. Begin with simple, uncomplicated togetherness. Find things you can do together—side by side. It might be refinishing old furniture or playing tennis or taking French lessons or joining a camera club or whatever interests you. You may want to try something new together. Or one of you may have to make some initial sacrifices in order to find common interests. Whatever you do should provide a meaningful togetherness where you can interact and enjoy each other. Christian couples should choose some service that both can become absorbed in—a home Bible study, perhaps, or a church ministry that can be carried out together. In the busyness of our culture, couples need to give their time in areas that bring them together, not fragment their relationship. If you presently are expanding your energies on projects that take you in opposite directions, you should change your projects.

Shared time, shared activities, shared interests, and shared experiences lead to shared feelings and shared confidences. "This was the cream of marriage," Jan Struther said, "this nightly turning out and sharing of the day's pocketful of memories." Andre Maurois defined a happy marriage as "a long conversation that always seems too short."

During this phase you will learn to trust each other—a critical factor in *phileo*. In a survey of more than 40,000 Americans conducted by *Psychology Today*, these qualities were most valued in a friend: (1) the ability to keep confidences; (2) loyalty; (3) warmth and affection. These are the qualities you must communicate to each other, and this will lead to a sense of openness between you that draws you into the next phase. As you move into a deeper level of sharing you take with you the growing joy of being together.

The rapport phase has been reached when you are ready to share aspects of yourself that are precious and vulnerable. Not only are you ready, but it becomes real joy to share yourself with your partner. Craig Massey has defined love as "that deliberate act of giving one's self to another so that the other person constantly receives enjoyment. Love's richest reward comes when the object of love responds to the gift." This is what you begin to experience and when it happens, you don't just *like* to be together anymore. You *love* to be with each other. *Phileo* is well under way!

The rapport phase is a time for sharpening communication skills. The complaint I hear most frequently is from the wife who desires to share her inmost thoughts while the husband feels uncomfortable doing so, usually because he has never found it easy to express himself. Difficulties can be overcome with practice in the rapport phase as couples learn to confide in each other and begin to see how rewarding and fulfilling it can be.

Because women usually feel more need to talk than men, husbands should learn that they can love their wives just by listening. I mean real listening: concentration accompanied by eye contact. Dr. Ross Campbell recommends focused attention as a major means of building love in a relationship. Husband, this means giving your wife your full, undivided attention so that she feels without question that she is completely loved; that she is valuable enough in her own right to warrant your appreciation and regard.

Through the operation of *phileo*, two separate selves begin to merge and mesh together as you develop a rapport—a harmonious oneness. At the same time this friendship love gives the assurance that you both are unique and valuable individuals. According to the laws of human behavior, this will cause you to become more lovable and even more free to love in return.

As you become practiced in rapport love, its joy will sweep you into the most mature phase of friendship where a willingness to learn more about your partner becomes an eagerness to know the beloved completely and to be as close as possible. The movement of *phileo* through these phases could be likened to a wheel rolling along, picking up speed. As the momentum builds, the pleasures of togetherness increase, closeness becomes a way of life, and cherishing your partner is now a reality, not just a wedding promise.

"I think a man and a woman should choose each other for life," J. B. Yeats said, "for the simple reason that a long life is barely enough for a man and woman to understand each other; and to understand is to love."

Married partners will agree that understanding each other is a lifelong process. It requires sensitivity, a quality developed as a part of total loving. To be sensitive is to be aware of your lover as a whole person; to recognize your beloved's uniqueness; and to discern what will best meet your mate's needs.

In the revelation phase both partners are freely open to one another. Both have gladly exchanged the original state of independence for an emotional interdependence that is unafraid to lean, to trust, and to seek fulfillment of personal needs and desires. On this level, both the needs and longings of the two personalities are understood and met in a process that becomes almost as natural as breathing.

Always remember that friendship requires attention. It must have something to feed on and respond to. Ask yourself and your partner: What are we overlooking that could make our relationship better? If we are a bit bored, what are we doing to add zest to our friendship?

Any marriage can benefit from more *phileo*. Since this friendship is a living entity, it must constantly grow or it will begin to wither. So think of tangible things you can do to help it grow.

Cherishing! It never happens quickly. As the middle-aged couple with six children said, "Love is what you've been through with somebody." But two of you cooperating can bring this cherishing about, slowly, beautifully, like the unfolding of a flower. ●

Whoso Findeth a Wife Findeth a Good Thing by Jane B. Sorenson

Who can find a suitable suburban wife, for her worth is far above secretary or cleaning woman?

The heart of her husband doth safely trust in her whether with eligible bachelor or high-pressure salesman.

She accepteth her husband as he is and hangeth up pajamas all the days of her life.

She seeketh new furniture but settleth for old and antiqueth it with her hands.

She runneth not out of milk and bringeth her food from afar, not just stores giving Green Stamps.

She decorateth her home in best of taste but showeth not emphasis on materialism.

Her family feeleth house can be "lived in"; yet it suddenly becometh immaculate when doorbell ringeth.

She riseth also when the alarm goeth off and dresseth, maketh breakfast and packeth lunches while family is still inserting contact lenses.

She girdeth her arms with strength and on Tuesday carryeth out leaves and tree prunings to street for disposal pick-up.

She cooketh ample meals, yet avoideth for teenagers chocolate, nuts, chewy foods, raw celery and, for husband, high cholesterol. She forgetteth not to defrost dinner.

When wearing last year's knit dress and ancient coat, she looketh like a million dollars.

She openeth her mouth with wisdom but knoweth when to keep it shut. She talketh seldom about trivia and never during football games.

She forgetteth not to make appointments for annual checkups, orthodontists, eye doctor, hair cuts and rabies shots.

She attendeth all meetings, singeth in choir, spendeth time to become friends with non-Christian neighbors, cooketh meals for sick, teacheth Bible class—but never becometh tired or cross and looketh well to the ways of her own household.

Her children never rise up to wonder why they have no clean socks or underwear.

She becometh not "obsolete" as husband becometh known at the gates. But, if his position riseth not, she remaineth content.

When husband spendeth week at Los Angeles gates, she panics not. She moppeth basement floor; she ordereth new water heater; she maketh papier-mâché log cabin for son's social studies project; she consoleth daughter snubbed by senior boy. And when, with family finally tucked into bed, she heareth phone ring, she reporteth to husband that "everything's fine."

She buyeth salt for the water softener and gently remindeth husband to bring it in, but the furnace filters she cleaneth herself.

She knoweth not how to raise hood of automobile, but yet she haveth oil changed, shock absorbers checked and tires rotated.

Give her a card on Mother's Day; and let her own works praise her in the gates.

Many wives do a pretty fair job, but thou, oh modern mom, excellest them all. ●

Have You Loved Your Child Today? by Rita Carver

In today's world one might wonder if mother is not headed for extinction. Preschools, day-care centers, and Big Bird all seem to assure us that they can do as good a job of raising our children as we can. Some of our feminist sisters have declared that as non-working mothers we are only maids doing the job that any eight-year-old could accomplish.

Turning to Scripture for a biblical perspective on motherhood, we find a seeming simplistic treatment of the topic. Paul instructs older women to teach the younger women to love their children (Titus 2:3,4). I used to wonder why Paul would instruct mothers to do something which should come so naturally—until one of those special creatures was added to our home! I had been a working wife who was used to deadlines, finished projects, and a feeling of accomplishment. With young David there are always deadlines, but never finished projects, and never a feeling of accomplishment. I began to struggle with some basic questions. What indeed is the purpose of a mother? Is she there merely to wash, cook, feed, and eternally change diapers?

The facts of the child's development are clear. In two decades, my tiny bundle of potential will be an emotionally, physically, intellectually, and spiritually independent individual. In only six short years, the majority of his adult behavior patterns will be firmly implanted. I wonder about the accomplishment of such enormous tasks. What part does a mother play in the process?

God says our purpose as mothers is to *love* our children. Did you see that in Titus? That is why God created mommies. That is the "how" of helping our children grow from dependent infants into mature adults. That is how we meet their basic needs of self-worth and intimacy with others. We need to love our children.

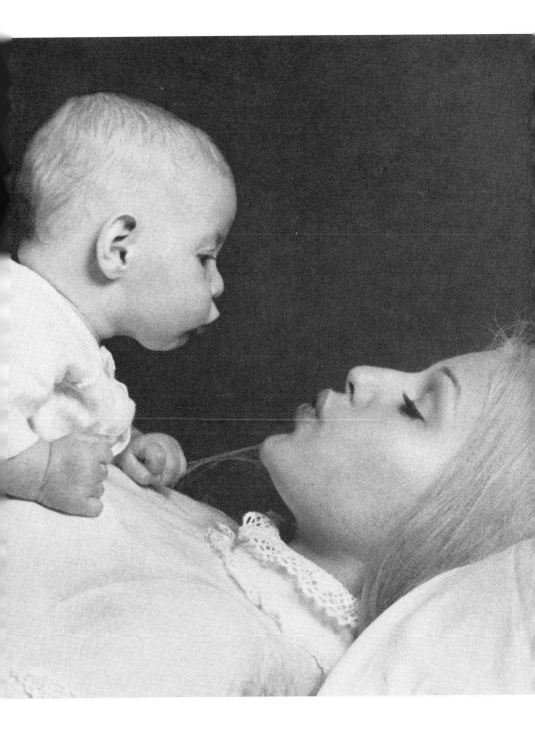

Love in this case does not mean that we simply do not beat our children nor that we meet all their physical needs. Paul uses the word for love which conveys the idea of friendship, positive feelings, and enjoyment. We are to enjoy our children, be their friend, and have positive feelings toward them.

As a mother, I know how difficult it is to enjoy one's children 24 hours a day. Sometimes children seem bent on destroying their mothers. No one is yelled at as much as a preschooler's mother. The newborn infant never seems pleased with mother's performance and tells her so. The two-year-old disapproves of mother's decisions and puts on a three-ring circus to communicate his displeasure. The four-year-old exhausts mother with constant requests, and the six-year-old questions her to death. How do we go about learning to enjoy our children?

The basis for this enjoyment is found in enjoying ourselves and our role as mothers. God has a very special purpose in giving you the children that you have. He is not only using us to shape our children's lives, he is also using our children to refine *our* lives.

God made us mothers because he has some things to teach us through the lives of our children—about love, life, patience, perspective, values, and empathy. While in everything we do we are teaching our children, in the mirror of their lives we can also gain a clearer picture of ourselves.

The greatest hindrance to enjoying ourselves and our role as mothers is the guilt trap of feeling that we are inadequate mothers. Most of our feelings of inadequacy are based on an unrealistic view of motherhood. Two myths cloud our concept of our God-given role.

The first is the mother martyr myth. Somehow we have gotten the impression that once we become mothers, we no longer have needs—that the children must always come first. This faulty thinking leads to resentment of our children, feelings of anger toward them, impatience, and eventually guilt at being such a poor, always-yelling mother. The same faulty thinking produces a child who feels he is worth nothing because he always makes mother angry.

As mothers we have certain basic needs that must be met. We need time away from the responsibilities of the home and the children. We need the support and encouragement of other adults. Too often this need for support falls solely on the husband, who then has no one to whom he can turn for support. We also need time alone with our husbands. In short, we need to attend to and take time for ourselves in order to better meet the demands of our children.

A second myth about motherhood is the super mom myth. In today's world we always seem to be looking for the super athlete, the super beauty queen, and even the super mom. But not even today's children need infallible mothers; they need real moms who are unafraid to let their children see them as they really are.

Let's look at some of the advantages of being fallible, human mothers. Consider typical statements like these:

"Mom, I'm afraid of the dark. Are you ever afraid?"

"Mom, Jimmy hit me. I hate him."

"Mom, I lost my book. What should I do?"

We can empathize with these emotional statements because we are human mothers who make mistakes, have fears, and sometimes fail. Some days we may have to spend a lot of time telling them, "I'm sorry; I was wrong."

Our children need to see us as we really are, not the facade we have erected and called "mother." As we live openly and honestly with ourselves and with our children, we can begin enjoying ourselves and our role as mothers.

Once we have gained some insight into the way we view ourselves as mothers, we need to know how we can enjoy our children. First, we need to learn to love our children unconditionally. A child, in order to be secure, needs to know and feel that someone loves him no-matter-what, and God has delegated that someone to be mom. We need to love our children when they are naughty, when they embarrass us, when they are sick—always! Just as God loves us unconditionally, we need to love our children in the same way, allowing them the same freedom to make mistakes and to fail that God has given to us.

Second, we need to learn to love and enjoy our children so that they *feel* loved. Ross Campbell lists three practical things we must do in order to make our children feel loved. We must give them eye contact, physical contact, and focused attention. (*How to Really Love Your Child*, Victor Books).

Third, we need to love and enjoy our children as *people*, possessing all the basic needs that we have but without the sufficient skills to communicate their needs adequately. Misbehavior becomes a child's primary means of communicating his needs because it gets mother's attention faster than anything else.

When our son consistently misbehaves, I am learning to ask, "What need do you have that I am not meeting?" Rather than "Why don't you do what I say?" I have been amazed at how disobedience becomes obedience when I put myself in his place, feel what he is feeling, and then meet the need that he is experiencing.

Children love to do adult, "real" things. We should be open to letting them try things rather than thinking "they're too little." At 20 months, our little one was pushing a mop, kneading bread dough, dusting, vacuuming in one place, and digging in the garden. Yes, it took me longer to accomplish my tasks, but I was enjoying my son and he was feeling important.

So where do we begin loving our children? With the routine of today—by making time for them! We can swing, walk, talk, listen, play, and work with the children God has given us. We are not wasting time. We are accomplishing our God-given task as mothers—loving our children. ●

Housewife on Holy Ground by Jane Fader

My attention was caught recently by these words of E. B. Browning:
And every common bush afire with God;
And only he who sees takes off his shoes
The rest sit around it and pluck blackberries.

I was intrigued by the idea that God is all around us and we are constantly on holy ground, but few of us realize it. We consistently pass up the "burning bush" experience of life because we see only the commonplace, and we react accordingly. At the moments when we should be "taking off our shoes" in acknowledgment of the presence of God in our lives, we are sitting down and eating blackberries—doing those things which satisfy our physical and emotional needs, but which in no way increase our awareness of God.

I went back to the story of Moses and the burning bush in the third chapter of Exodus to try to discover some truth for my own life out of his experience. Moses' encounter with God at that time involved his recognition of something unusual in his ordinary surroundings. God was there with a message and a mission for Moses, and the startled servant was directed to take off his shoes to acknowledge the presence of God.

I wonder how many times in my seemingly humdrum life as a housewife and mother I pass by holy ground and never realize it. I believe holy ground is any place where we stand and become aware of the presence of God in our lives. The opportunities are endless, but how often do we see and worship? Aren't we much more prone to sit down and pick the berries?

When my youngest child comes to me with a scratch or with hurt feelings from some minor incident with his friends, I suppose I feel that I am on safe ground. I feel fairly competent to handle the physical problems, even priding myself on being able to remain calm when a real crisis arises. When hurt feelings are involved, I soothe and reassure, knowing children forgive and forget quickly. Yes, I feel that I am on safe ground.

My reaction is quite the opposite when my teenager approaches me with some of his problems. When I am confronted with his boy-girl relationships, his rebellion against adult authority, his search for his own identity, and all the new emotions which accompany his changing voice and hair on his chest, I feel that I am on shaky ground. I find it unexplainably difficult to relate to him, and I fear my responses are feeble.

So with my children I find myself on either safe ground or shaky ground; but do I ever stop and realize I am on *holy* ground? How often could I use their experiences, their problems, their disappointments to teach them something of the loving concern of God for each of his children? How often have I failed to teach them the value of prayer, simply because I did not think to suggest that we take a matter to God together? The opportunities to show my children how God relates to them are as abundant and varied as are their life situations, but I too often keep on my shoes of practicality and eat the berries of child psychology, while holy ground slips away.

As I consider my life as a housewife and neighbor relating to other women day after day, I fear I do not see the "burning bush" experiences in these relationships. When a neighbor comes in for a cup of coffee and spills out her frustrations, fears, or distress, I feel that I am now on common ground. I am understanding, I am sympathetic, I say "I know exactly how you feel because I've felt that way, too." I establish common ground because I think it will help this woman to know she is not alone in how she feels; but I do not look twice and see that I am also on *holy* ground.

I think it is important for me, as a Christian, to admit to my humanness as I relate to other women. I should let them know that I have problems, temptations, doubts, and anxieties just as they do; but I should not stop with establishing common ground. I must move on to holy ground by telling them that through my life with Christ, I have found the strength and help I need to face these human difficulties. When women choose to confide in me and trust me with those small but significant portions of their lives, I should use the opportunity to direct their thoughts toward God. But I tend to keep on my shoes of humanness and sit and eat the berries of sympathetic understanding, while holy ground remains unheeded.

As a wife, I should realize that marriage is certainly holy ground; but it too easily becomes a battleground! I am bombarded with literature that tells me open communication is the answer to my marital problems, but seldom am I told exactly how to accomplish that goal. If I stop to see my Christian husband as the bush aglow with the fire of God in my own life, would it be as easy for me to be critical of him? Would I be as tempted to nag, ridicule, or ignore him if I viewed our marriage as holy ground?

It seems almost ridiculous to need to point out our church as holy ground, but I wonder how often I view it that way when I am trying to work with other church people. As I try to get a job done which I feel is important a great number of frustrations and hostilities can develop. Rather than seeking out the people against whom I feel resentment, and making a holy ground of our turning to God to help heal our strained relationships, I may start a burial ground, which I fill with bitterness against God's own people.

As I become increasingly aware that "earth's crammed with heaven, and every common bush afire with God," I believe that every area of my life is potentially holy ground. My problem is learning to identify the particular moments when the "burning bush" is right at my feet. I am trying to do this by becoming sensitive to each person around me, sensitive to each situation I encounter, and sensitive to God's presence always with me. I am attempting to discover those times when I can especially sense God's nearness and recognize the opportunity to demonstrate his realness and his relatedness to each of us by what I say or do. I am asking God daily to make me willing to take off my shoes on the holy ground of daily living, and help me spend less of my life merely "plucking blackberries." ●

Wives: This is Your Life by Maryanna W. Johnson

Women have individual needs and talents as well as feminine ones. Whereas a man's life is divided into two phases: (1) preparation for his task in the world (2) performance of that task, a woman has three phases: (1) preparation for a role in her home and a role in the world (2) life at home, nurturing growing children (3) life in the world when the children are grown and gone. Even if she has a job during that second stage, the responsibility of caring for the family rests most heavily on her shoulders.

But much of the current literature about married women seems to ignore this three-fold division of their lives. Either women are assured that they can take jobs just like men (and have a husband and children on the side), or else they are urged to take more delight in hearth and home, and leave the world of ideas and skills to men.

It is possible, however, for a woman to have room in her life for both worlds, though she may not manage both in equal amounts. In the second phase of life, the maternal role predominates; in the third phase of life the individual role can come to the fore. At all times, a woman has the capacity for both.

This duality can be frustrating or enriching, depending upon how it is handled. During the second stage of her life, a young mother's individuality may add either a sour note or a grace note to her family. Some of the happiest children have mothers who reserve an hour a day during nap-time for reading or painting, or who devote an afternoon a week to some stimulating activity away from home.

During the third stage of life, a mature woman can either give in to depression as her children depart, or she can learn to envelop a wider circle with her natural warmth and understanding.

How well a woman handles the second and third stages of life depends on how well she prepared herself during the first stage;

here many women have sold themselves short. Girls who have prepared both for a role at home and in the world possess inner resources with which to meet the challenges and limitations inherent in each of these capacities.

But women who are having difficulty because of poor preparation can still remedy their situation if they really want to. If you are a "trapped housewife" who finds she has no time to herself, or a lonely lady who fears she has no gift to offer to others, stop bemoaning your fate and begin to work out a program which will help you deal with these dilemmas. As a woman, your goal will be to discover your individual role in society; as a Christian, your goal will be to find your function in the Body of Christ. Very likely, these two will blend into one.

The opportunities and privileges God has given a wife and mother must not be regarded lightly. One's husband and children are her first consideration. But this does not necessitate a total neglect of one's individuality and God-given talents. It isn't either-or, it's both . . . each in its own time.

As you set out to discover your gift, you must first realize that you have one. Everybody is special in some way; no one is without a gift. Of course, some women are more clever or attractive than others, but the point is that there is a vast variety in the members constituting the Body of Christ, and we are all needed, no matter how insufficient we feel ourselves to be.

Perhaps the woman who fears she has no gift has spent too much time envying a person with prominent talents, and has not recognized that even the best brains or the loveliest eyes could never do the work of common parts like elbows, knuckles or toes. Your job is not to argue with God about the qualities He didn't give you, but to use your gift—after you find it. Finding it will take time and effort, but if you persevere you will discover that God has been seeking you to commit into your hands a ministry which only you can perform.

Three things are of crucial importance in your search for a ministry of your own: knowing God, knowing yourself, and knowing the world you live in.

Perhaps you are a solitary soul, rich in communion but never reaching out to other people. Perhaps you are trying hard to help others when you yourself have serious, unsolved problems. Or perhaps you have never perceived the realities around you except in a limited way; possibly the full dimensions of God's world have never dawned on you—its beauty and its ugliness; its fresh young faces and gnarled old ones; its joys and its pain; the vastness and stillness under the stars; the challenge of modern mathematics; the lessons of history and biography; the perfection of a single poem or painting. God created a world of endless variety and complexity . . . do you know what His world is like?

After you have evaluated your relationship to God, your knowledge of yourself and your awareness of the world, the next step is to make plans for improving where you are weak. If your lack is spiritual, your pastor should be able to help you. If you need guidance on how to grow in the other areas, some of the suggestions in the accompanying box may awaken you to the world around you and the possibilities within you. If a suggestion attracts you, this tells you something about yourself, and is worth following up to see where it leads. Afterward, add ideas of your own; even if you never carry out all your projects, just writing them down will help you to become alert and inventive and receptive to new ways of thinking and doing.

The process of learning to understand yourself and your world is neither quick nor easy; it requires persistence and a willingness to be different from others when necessary.

If you are a young mother on a limited budget, it will take courage to hire a sitter so that you can have an afternoon to wander off by yourself. If you are older and "distracted with much serving" as Martha was, it will take courage to drop some activity in order to find time to decide whether you have been responding to His call or simply yielding to human pressures.

As you persist, and pray, and work through your list, and grow in awareness of yourself and others and life in general, sooner or later something in you will dove-tail with something in the world around you and you will know "this is it."

As you become more and more free to be yourself rather than a poor carbon copy of someone else, you will be glad that you have parted with sterile routines and a rigid outlook, and have become flexible and open and adventurous. It is exhilarating to break out of the bondage of doing only what is expected of you, and to let God lead you into His ministry for you. ●

Suggestions for discovering your talents

(1) Walk around in your church building some day during the week when it is empty; ask yourself, what little thing in this place needs doing that I could do? (A surprising number of seminary-trained pastors spend hours duplicating the bulletin, changing the lettering on the sign, setting mousetraps and supplying paper in the washroom!)

(2) Make a list of unanswered questions which have troubled you about life, about God, about the Bible. Is there any provision in the life of your congregation for adults to talk freely about such things? If not, could you be instrumental in starting a discussion group, or a special course in doctrine by the pastor?

(3) Read about some of the interesting things women are doing which might appeal to you (missionary magazines and your daily paper are a good source of this kind of information): caring for a foster child, working with migrants, duplicating and mailing prayer letters for a missionary, "adopting" and corresponding with a foreign orphan, doing volunteer work in a hospital, assisting with the recreation program of a home for the aging or a school for delinquents, participating in a local women's political organization.

(4) Browse in the public library, not to find anything in particular, but to see what is there. Look through a magazine you have never seen before. Take out a book on a subject you never read about before. Find out if records or films or paintings can be borrowed as well as books; borrow some.

(5) Cultivate the acquaintance of someone you often see but whom you have not considered to be "your type"; this person might open up to you a whole new world of interest and need.

(6) The next time you have coffee with your friends, stop talking and just look and listen. What is there in these women that you never saw before? What hidden griefs or struggles are betrayed by their faces? In what ways could they be contributing and achieving instead of vegetating in their daily ruts and routines? How many of them are going through the same struggle you are, but have no one with whom they feel free to discuss it?

(7) Take a leisurely walk around your neighborhood some afternoon and think about the families in these homes. Do you know them only too well, or not at all? What are the needs and interests of these people? Could you be a more meaningful part of their lives in some way?

One Mother's Choice by Bonnie Angel

As a working mother, I began to wonder about my situation. The Lord admonishes me to be a good steward of the talents he has given me. How should I handle an ability that is salable in the career market, when he has also given me children at home?

I knew that there are times when women must work. But what of women who work for a second income? It may mean a new car, a summer vacation, a new wardrobe, or ham sandwiches instead of peanut butter. None of these reasons is particularly worldly.

I have four children, and for years I worked. There was a time when it was a necessity, but then I continued because it had become a pattern of life and I couldn't imagine how we would get along without my salary.

But it seemed that everything I read would point out problems that stemmed from a woman's absence from home. One day in his sermon our pastor mentioned that a little child sitting on the floor playing with his blocks isn't impressed that his father is out late making $50,000 a year for him. He is only impressed if his father is on the floor playing with him. Naturally, I substituted "mother" into this statement and heard a message loud and clear.

Then I read a short message by Peter Marshall called "Keepers of the Springs." The words rang in my ears: "The modern challenge to motherhood is the eternal challenge—that of being godly women. . . . We hear about . . . beautiful women, smart women, sophisticated women, career women, talented women . . . but so seldom do we hear of a godly woman. . . . I believe women come nearer fulfilling their God-given function in the home than anywhere else."

At this time in my personal devotions I was studying the book of Luke. Chapter 12 asks, "Who then is the faithful and wise manager, whom the master puts in charge of his servants to give them their food allowance at the proper time?" This text turns out to be pretty descriptive of motherhood. I pondered . . . my Master is God. I am training my children to be his servants. Then I read, "It will be good for that servant whom the master finds doing so when he returns."

I am to receive God's favor for keeping on with the task at hand, being a good steward of his servants. This Scripture goes on to describe the advantages and disadvantages of doing what the Master puts in our charge. It warns us not to slack off because we think it will be a long time before Jesus returns. I tried to evaluate my reasons for working. I weighed what I was gaining by what I was giving up. Would the condition of my job or the condition of my children be more important if I knew Jesus would return in one year?

The inner conviction grew until I knew that I had to act. I was a successful businesswoman. I had reached several new plateaus for women in my field. The temptation to stay was great.

I discussed my feelings and conclusions with my husband, and we prayed about it together. We discussed the things that we as a family would be forced to give up without my income. It was not a simple decision. But I gave my notice at work and began to ease out of my responsibilities.

That was a year and a half ago. Life has not been a bed of roses, but looking back, there have been many more blessings and positive achievements than negative ones. The time has flown by, and I smile as I recall many of the things that I have learned.

Those first few moments when the children come home from school are so dramatic: the breathless account of the mean dog down the street that they worried about . . . the pride of accomplishment in the papers they hold tightly in their fists . . . the time of debate and analytical discussion over their teachers' seemingly unfair actions. Each day I become better acquainted with my children's thoughts, questions, and needs.

The most noticeable need for my presence at home has come from my teenagers. After being home for a short time, I received a comment from our son that dynamically assured me that I was where I belonged. I had given him some minor instruction, and he snapped back, "I've already raised myself. Why are you trying to tell me what to do now?"

It wasn't a pleasant thing to hear, but it halted thoughts of going back to work for a few years!

An unexpected problem flowed gradually into my life and almost drowned me before I realized what was happening. When people find that you are not working, they think you have time for everything, and you can easily become busier than when you were working. I had to learn to say "no"!

Each age group has been able to inspect the new generation and say, "Things aren't as they used to be," but I am appalled at the variety of attractions that are offered to children today. Children, like all of us, look for somewhere to be loved and needed. This warmth can be counterfeited at the game center, the bowling alley, the school playground, the park, or in the van parked down the street. I am more convinced than ever that it takes a mother's full-time giving of love, encouragement, and support to come close to competing with what the world offers.

Another thing that I always thought I needed was the challenge of the career world. Now I have found that balancing the budget on one income instead of two takes all the skill, planning, and effort of any full-time job. A text that has sustained me through many dark moments this year comes from Matthew 6 where I am told to lay up my treasures in heaven and not on earth. Devoting ourselves to our homes and families is definitely a step in laying up treasures in heaven. And even though our tithe is smaller now, I like to think that Jesus is blessing it and multiplying it as he did the loaves and fishes.

I know that as a Christian I am admonished to be active in fighting for the right. A marvelous place to start is at my own address! ●

Housewifeitis is Spreading by Myrna Grant

Ruth dropped the blackened saucepan into the sink and collapsed onto the nearest chair in tears. Maybe it was because she had scorched the pudding. Or perhaps it was because of the battle she had had with Tommy, aged three, who had insisted on wearing snowboots to bed for his nap. It certainly didn't help that she had been up twice in the night with the baby.

But in her heart Ruth knew her despair was the result of more than a bad day. Even good days found her depressed and restless. Until her talk with Peggy, she had wondered if she were the only Christian homemaker who felt this way.

But Peggy, her friend since college, felt the same. This discovery had come when Peggy, now a mother of four, had said over coffee, "I feel discontented all the time. I never have devotions anymore. Not really. I'm too rushed or too tired. And on the top of it all, I'm bored. I need to get away from the house."

Ruth and Peggy were alike in many ways. After graduation both had held interesting jobs and had been active and happy in the church. Both had entered marriage with zest and had welcomed their children as blessings from God. But Ruth hadn't quite agreed with Peggy's decision to get a part-time job.

Though Ruth felt she was in as much of a rut as Peggy, what bothered her more than boredom was that her daily routine seemed identical to that of her neighbors. She tried to explain how she felt to her husband.

"We do the same housework, teach our children the same things—honesty, courtesy, kindness, and all that. We mow the lawn, drive to the supermarket, and bring in the evening paper." She paused for breath and then resumed hurriedly as she saw her husband's answer forming.

"I know we're Christians, and we try to teach the children about God. But lots of our neighbors do that, too, even when they don't go to church themselves. Life just seems such an anticlimax—so Peggy's getting a job."

Ted, used to withholding judgment, only commented: "She's pretty busy already, isn't she?"

The weeks passed, bringing disappointment. Peggy's job didn't work out. It provided an outlet for her interests, but the demands on her time were more than she had expected. Her schedule was relentless and any mixup—a sick child at breakfast or a late babysitter—could be disastrous. She became exhausted and frantic. The delight of working again was spoiled by her fatigue, and there was now no time at all in her day for God. Eventually she quit working.

"The worst part of it," Peggy told Ruth grimly, "was that as a Christian I felt worse and worse. If life seemed tedious at home, it was even emptier at work. After the novelty wore off I was more of a slave to the clock than ever. It was all so much meaningless activity. I sure don't understand it. We've both read so much about what a lift a part-time job can be to the homemaker. Some lift!"

Peggy's job experience was a letdown to Ruth. She had been hoping that Peg's answer might work for her, too.

"You two are a fine pair!" Ted had joshed. "But at least you're not another Mary Moore."

Ruth nodded. They had been praying for Mary for months. An active church member all her life, Mary had been one of the most popular young matrons in church. But when children came, Mary had to leave a teaching career and stay home. The change in her was startling. Her bitterness seemed to spring up overnight. Year by year her resentment deepened. Finally she stopped attending church. Her depression and anger, results of the feeling that life had cheated her, were making her marriage and home a nightmare.

The more Ruth thought about her own dissatisfactions, the more convinced she became that there must be many troubled homemakers. She eventually decided to visit her pastor.

"Now don't tell me I'm just tired, Pastor Taylor, because I'm not! Not that I don't get exhausted, mentally and physically, but a good night's sleep cures that! My problem is that I feel 'let down' about life, as if I'm a drudge and that's all. And I don't know what I should do about it."

"It's a common thing for homemakers to feel discontented," he replied. "The world looks pretty big when you see it from a kitchen window—especially when you know you could be 'out there' doing something. You're right when you say life must be more than endless routine for a Christian."

He smiled as he continued: "I wonder why Christian mothers don't realize how basically different they are from their nonbelieving neighbors?"

"Different? Why, that's what depressed me the most. We're not a bit different," Ruth exclaimed.

"A lot of American housewives get part-time jobs and love it," Pastor Taylor replied. "If Christians are the same as nonbelievers, why didn't this help your friend Peggy?"

"I don't know. She said something about it making life more meaningless."

"Here's where the important difference lies, Ruth. If a woman is not a Christian, she can interpret her dissatisfaction as a rebellion against the drudgery, as you call it, of housework and child care. She can get a job, interest herself in hobbies or community projects, and often she feels much better about herself."

"But that doesn't work for a Christian?"

Pastor Taylor fingered his Bible thoughtfully. "I don't think the Christian mother necessarily can be refreshed by outside work. Different activity may not be what she needs. Her restlessness may not respond to diversion because her sense of worth depends on her relationship to God, not to herself."

Ruth began to listen intently.

"We hear so much about the dilemma of the American woman and her changing role in society. Christian women are part of this 'dilemma.' But there is a God-factor in a believing woman's life that changes the picture for her. How creative or successful such a woman feels is not enough to really satisfy her. It is God she really cares about, and what he wants of her. Don't you agree?"

Ruth nodded. "What you're saying, then, is that a Christian mother might be restless about her relationship to God and mistake it for the general discontent a lot of American women are experiencing?"

"That's it. Naturally there isn't one norm for all Christian mothers.

Women never fit into a formula. But I would think that a mother ought to first be sure that her spiritual life was blooming before she decided that housekeeping and the children were getting her down."

Ruth laughed with a sense of relief she had not felt for months. "I can't tell you how much insight you've given me. I've been putting housekeeping first and neglecting God and the values I care most about. No wonder I felt depressed."

They prayed together, and as Ruth walked home she anticipated the days ahead. It wouldn't be easy to change her daily pattern of rush and routine. But determination that she wouldn't let housework cheat her again would help.

Perhaps instead of looking for a single period long enough to have devotions, she would manage several short intervals. Even rising a little earlier would give her extra leisure to seek God.

And Ruth's heart surged with joy as she thought of the spiritual nurture she would give her children in the unfolding years ahead. The distinctive role of a Christian mother had never been clear to her before. She felt her own relationship to God kindle as she remembered the pastor's final words: "Keep thinking of that hoped-for day when you will stand before God and say: 'Behold, I and the children you have given me. . . .' " ●

Faith Tested Our Marriage by June Williams

Nine years ago, an overwhelming change came into my life: I became a Christian. I was no longer the same woman who had said "I do" five years earlier. I had a different outlook, new hopes, new desires, and a new interpretation of right and wrong. And I wondered if my husband and I could, or even should, continue living together.

Mac appeared hostile about my decision. He was confused, frustrated, and often angry. While I understood his resentment at my choosing another above him, I could not alter my course. Our communications dropped almost to zero, but somehow we formed an unspoken agreement: we would try to "stick it out."

Sticking it out was not an easy task for either of us. As with many new Christians, I was unsure about how I was expected to act. Mac was definitely a big hindrance to my attempts at righteous living. His sins seemed to be hanging out all over, and I feared he was dragging our children straight to hell!

Fortunately, that stage passed quickly (although not too quickly for Mac!). From self-righteousness, I moved into martyrdom. Some of my church friends helped me along by reminding me of how rough I had it. Mac shut me out of his private life entirely. I guess it's no wonder; my best response to his needs was tainted with long-suffering tolerance.

The result of my actions and Mac's withdrawal was a severe emotional separation. We remained together in body, but it was as if our souls had filed for divorce. It is incredibly lonely to be married to a stranger!

I reached bottom at this point, and in my desperation I turned to God. As I prayed over many months, I became more and more convinced that God could save our marriage, and I began to trust him to do just that.

I started studying God's Word, and it became clear to me that I had the wrong concept of what a wife should be. The Bible portrays a wife as her husband's helper, his confidante, his gentle advisor. The contrast between the "virtuous woman" (Prov. 31:10) and me was as the difference between day and night!

The Lord also clarified my understanding of submission. I learned that submission is an attitude of respect for another, not a debasing of oneself. My fear of becoming a "doormat" was totally unfounded, as long as I maintained some measure of self-worth.

Best of all, God adjusted my focus. In my desire to rid my husband of his faults, I had forgotten his good points. The Lord reintroduced me to Mac's wisdom, integrity, and steadfast loyalty. I began to see him in a new light. True, he was not a man of God, but he was a good man, a good husband, and a good father. I thanked God for showing me the worth of our relationship before it was too late to save it.

Once I became willing to work at preserving our marriage, my prayers took a new direction. I found that I was no longer praying for my husband to be changed. Now I prayed, "God, change me." I was the one whose actions had threatened to destroy our marriage; now I desired its restoration.

During all those months of instability, Mac's determination to stay with me never wavered. The quality in him which I admire as loyalty, he defines as stubbornness. He was not about to discard our future together, just because a change had taken place.

His main anxiety, at first, was that I would try to convert him. But God had graciously granted me the wisdom to keep quiet on that subject. When Mac realized he had nothing to fear in that respect, he began to relax a little. He was still aware of my unspoken disapproval of him, but his loyalty (or stubbornness) endured even that.

When I began to practice my newfound love for him, he reacted with suspicion. Cautiously, he accepted my peace offerings. Slowly, he started returning my love and respect. Our trust level crept up, and soon we were able to communicate again. Gradually, we found that our caring relationship was returning.

It has been over two years since God began to heal our marriage. The process has been slow but steady, and at times painful. Admitting past errors and asking forgiveness often hurts, but as we forgive and accept forgiveness our union grows stronger.

Mac and I still encounter problems common to every marriage. Also, we have occasional trials which are unique to our situation. But our determination to remain together puts our differences and difficulties in proper perspective.

I do not know whether Mac will choose to join me in following Jesus Christ, but we now know that our mutual love need not depend on mutual agreement. We can respect each other despite our differences. We are learning to love one another just as we are.

Nine years ago, I thanked God when my soul was born again. Today I thank him for the rebirth of my marriage! ●

What Mothers Are by Irene Steigerwald

Mothers can begin being mothers when they are around sixteen, and they sometimes keep it up until they are past eighty, which must make it about the longest career on record.

They come in all sizes, shapes, and colors, but don't be fooled; the tiny ones can pack a powerful punch, and the big ones can faint at the sight of a spider.

When vandals besieged Rome, it was a stately mother, who, when the despoilers demanded her jewels, placed an arm around her children and proclaimed: *Hic sunt ornamentis!* ("These are my jewels!")

A mother will scold quite hard when you pout for a party dress that costs fifty dollars. Then, just when you have resigned yourself to wearing the old blue tulle, she will dig down under the newspaper lining the top bureau drawer, and come up with five old ten-dollar bills, which she presses into your hand.

A mother will scream like a banshee at dirty dishes left in the sink, and then stay up until one A.M. baking the three cherry pies you promised for the bake sale.

In a recent newspaper account, a pretty young mother offered one of her eyes for an operation for her son, who was losing his sight. Said the hard-bitten old surgeon: "In the face of love like this, I stand speechless."

A mother will remain dry-eyed when Junior falls out of the apple tree and breaks an arm. She is not particularly moved at funerals or sad movies, but her eyes fill up when you come down the aisle in the beautiful white gown.

Mothers will ask fathers if they think mothers are getting fat, and when fathers say yes, then mothers get mad.

One mother whose little runaway boy was brought home by the

police got on her knees and hugged him tightly, and then got up and gave him the worst licking he ever had!

Mothers can remember the birthdays and anniversaries of all the aunts and cousins, but they forget who called you from the malt shop right after school.

Your mother will take a folded newspaper and give the dog a spanking for getting up on your bedspread. Then, when he gets a piece of glass in his paw, she drives him to the vet, ten miles away, and holds him on her lap while the vet fixes him.

You take one day a year to think especially about your mother; she takes three hundred and sixty-five to think about you.

But that's the way she wants it! ●

I'm a Career Mother by Mary L. Sherk

Politely I listened as my younger sister, newly married and embarked on a different life-style than mine, told me her plans.

"Children just aren't necessary for our relationship," she said. "We can do so much, both working. In two years we're going to Europe. Isn't that marvelous? I'm so glad I chose a high-paying career field."

I finished diapering my youngest child and looked about me. *Was she sorry for me?* I thought. The kitchen wallpaper needed replacing, but our daughter Lynn needed braces for her teeth. I remembered other pressing bills. The wallpaper would just have to be outdated a year or two more.

After another cup of coffee, my career-oriented sister left in her car with a cheerful wave of her hand. I intercepted Danny as he crawled purposefully toward my new potted palm. After all I'd gone through getting it to look just right, I didn't intend to let him ruin it.

As I herded Danny away and pointed him toward his toy box, my thoughts stayed with my sister. I realized motherhood wasn't in fashion with some young couples these days, as it was when I married. Many young women today feel motherhood is not for them.

It's not just the demands of motherhood they object to, either. They want rewarding and fulfilling lives. Well, so do I, naturally. It all sounds very attractive in the slick-paged magazines, on TV talk shows, and from my sister.

I thought of my own working life early in my marriage. Truthfully, I admitted, what I had was a job, not a career. Spending 20 or 30 years doing what I had done didn't seem appealing at all. I was happier being a stay-at-home wife and mother—wasn't I?

My job had not been particularly interesting. Of course, it might have led to something bigger and better. But I quit when I was pregnant, and I hadn't had a lot of extra time since then to wonder whether I had done the right thing.

It had been a paycheck I needed very much at the time. But it was a routine, often boring job. Apparently my work experience did not fall in the same category as my sister's.

My mind turned over thought after thought as I prepared Danny's lunch. He was beginning to slow down. I would feed him and put him down for his nap. Soon he was stowed peacefully in bed to renew his energy for an onslaught on the second half of his day.

There would be time to think about my missed career later. While I had a few quiet minutes, I needed to recruit 15 people to help with the spring school bazaar.

Forty calls later I turned wearily from the phone. My arm felt like it had a permanent kink and my mind whirled with tentative ideas for raising money—how to get the bazaar organized and make the most possible money for the school. If the slightest hint of my sister's ideas entered my head at that moment, they soon were drowned in my problems and in Danny's waking bright-eyed and lively from his nap.

Lynn and Wendy came home from school then, and it was much later that evening, when all three of the children were in bed, that I again had a spare moment.

I was tired and irritated, my mind occupied with the school bazaar. With so many mothers working, it was difficult to get volunteer help on projects. Responsibility for the whole affair rested squarely on my shoulders.

My sister's morning visit intruded again. What did I do all day, anyway? Had I forgotten how to put in a full day's work? Was I too content, letting my husband bear the full burden of providing for us financially? Was I fair to him?

I decided to write down all my activities during the next week. Maybe my sister was right. Maybe I should be out in the business world producing and contributing to society in a meaningful way. I borrowed a piece of notepaper from Wendy's three-ring notebook.

A week later I looked over my schedule.

There did seem to be time-slots when I did nothing at all. But, wait a minute . . . 3:45 to 4:30 on school days. That's when the girls get home and I begin making dinner so I can hear about their day.

If they didn't tell me what happened at school, who would they tell? The special moment might slip past unnoticed. Well, maybe it wasn't all that important.

But there was the day Wendy had not come home when expected. She just missed the first bus, I had thought. I called the school to see if there was an activity I hadn't remembered. Wendy wasn't there, they said. She got on her bus as usual.

I hung up the phone. Where could she be? The clock's hands crept around too quickly—she was now an hour and a half late. I couldn't wait any longer. It would be dark soon. I began calling her friends.

On the third try, I found her. "Yes, Wendy's here," a young voice said.

My body sagged in relief.

"Wendy?"

"Hi, Mom—is something wrong?"

"No. I wondered where you were. You didn't tell me where you were going." I tried to keep my voice even and unworried.

"Oh, I forgot, Mom. Shannon's mother said we could work on our social studies project at her house."

"Is Shannon's mother there now?"

"No, but her big sister is."

"How old is her big sister?"

"I don't know. Seventh grade, I think."

"Where's their mother?"

"At work. It's all right, Mom. We're watching TV while we do the project."

"You should have told me where you were going. It's all right. It was only that I didn't know."

"I'm sorry, Mom."

I didn't want to nag or hover over her. But I didn't like the idea of their being alone and unsupervised. It was one of the times—and I've had others—when a parent says a silent prayer of thanks that things turned out all right.

Later I solved the problem of Shannon by having Wendy invite her to our house for school projects.

How often I've thought of the millions of children who go home to empty houses after school because their mothers work. I don't want that for my children. And neither do I want to be an unpaid baby-sitter for children of working mothers; but I often am. If I don't do it, who will?

I found another time on my schedule when I was idle. After a moment I realized it was the time of day my husband arrives home. It's when he tells me what bothered him or what pleased him at work during the day.

It's his unwinding time, and I listen. I'm interested in his work, but I know, too, that he needs to get things off his chest. It's also the time I tell him how things went at home. I try not to greet him with a list of broken appliances and things gone wrong. Years ago I decided to try to give him good news first.

Other "empty" hours of my week were volunteer hours at the school, the hospital, and the church. Hours involved totaled considerably more than the 40 usually spent on a paid job.

Were those hours important? I thought so. Time tutoring slow learners at school was important. It could mean the difference between passing or failing for these children.

Then there's meal preparation time. I cut corners when I can, but I don't feed my family all convenience foods. So I put in extra time there, but I feel it's important to our general health.

My sister will live her own life, and I will live mine. Hers won't include sticky kisses or being needed by sick or frightened children. No first days of school or scheming to stretch the budget to include Christmas presents. But I wouldn't miss such moments for anything.

All those hours on my weekly schedule. Sometimes the tasks are routine, sometimes hectic. But so are paid jobs and careers. And back to the point: If I don't do it, who will? ●

I Married for Love Anonymous

I can only tell my story with the understanding that my name is kept secret, because what I'm going to say is different from what I tell my friends. What I say to relatives on my Christmas cards is what you're supposed to say when you've been married two and a half years and are still considered a bride: we're in love, we're happy, and life together is great. Occasionally I feel that way, but most of the time I don't.

You don't know how hard it is to admit that to somebody. A year ago I couldn't admit it to myself. I know things weren't going like I thought they should, that Dave, I'll call him, wasn't acting like he used to, and that I cried a lot. But still I kept thinking that things would work out. At first, all we needed, I said, were a few weeks to get the apartment organized. Then I said that all we needed was a little more money so it wouldn't be such a strain staying on our budget.

But now I've faced a fact I never believed before: people can act completely different in a new set of circumstances. That's the way it's been with Dave. And maybe that's the way it's been with me.

My cousin Marie was raised with me; she was three years older—beautiful and talented. I envied her more than I can tell, but she never included me in her circle of friends. I was always too young, too corny, too sloppy to go along.

I don't mean I was Cinderella or anything. I had my own friends, and Marie and I went our separate ways. Then when I was still a senior, I met Dave, who was nine years older than I. He was a college man, good looking, kind, and—what's more—interested in me, not Marie.

That's all it took. I was so sure Dave was meant for me that I banked everything I had on our marriage. Looking back, I can see how I thought it would solve all sorts of problems—my feeling of inferiority to Marie, and so on.

No one could talk me out of it, so everyone consented graciously. There was a big church wedding. Marie stood up with me, Dave smiled at me there at the altar as though I were the only woman in the world, and it was definitely the happiest moment of my life.

The ceremony lasted a few minutes, but a marriage is supposed to last a lifetime. I'd never thought about the everyday problems of living together. I was a romanticist when it came to marriage. Though I didn't dream about a cozy fireplace and a vine-covered cottage, I did fantasize Dave coming home from work and taking me in his arms—night after night after night.

That wasn't the way it was. Part of the time he was just as he'd always been—warm and passionate and good-humored—but there were others when he wanted to be by himself, or when he wanted serious talk about some business matter and didn't appreciate my stroking his hair. There were times when he wanted dinner immediately but I wanted to talk, or times when I'd be scrubbing the bathroom and he'd get an idea to go somewhere. It sounds so trivial, talking about it, but when it happened it wasn't small at all.

I'm just beginning to realize—and it's only because I've been having some marriage counseling—that it's not the things that cause trouble as much as our reactions to them. And Dave's not much more mature about this than I am. There were a lot of ways to handle that bit about cleaning the bathroom. There were a lot of different things I could have said. But instead I started crying about how he hadn't asked me out for three weeks, and only got around to it when I was filthy dirty and needed an hour to get ready. There were other problems involved, too—my resentment that we hadn't gone out earlier, my groundless suspicion that he didn't really want me along, and so on. It's never one problem, but a whole host of problems mixed up together, not the least of which were Dave's doubts about himself and my doubts about me, and our chronic need for reassurance that we were really loved.

Would I marry again at 18? I wouldn't admit it to Dave—but no. I thought I was so mature. I was a person who always took life seriously, and I thought I'd make a wonderful wife. I didn't know until I started in counseling that it's not mature to always hide your feelings as I did. I wasn't immature for my age; I was just immature for getting married.

Dave is in many respects a wonderful person, and I really hope the marriage works out. But I realize now he isn't the only person I could have married. If I'd had more dating experience—if I'd realized I was attractive after all, I wouldn't have jumped at the first nice man to come along. As it was, I needed Dave so badly to prove I could measure up to Marie that I confused it with the feeling that we were destined for each other.

Would I advise other kids to marry at 18? I know one girl who was 19 when she married, and as far as I know she's happy. But, of course, she thinks I'm happy too, so I can't be sure. There are six other friends who married at 17 and 18, and all six marriages are on the rocks.

If you are really "grown-up" at 18, you don't have to get married early. You're confident of yourself and your future without having to grab at things as though it's the last chance you may have. But if marriage looks like a chance to snuggle up on a rainy night and keep from being lonely, you let yourself in for a new kind of loneliness. When a gulf develops between you and the person you thought you loved, that must be one of the worst kinds of loneliness.

I suppose it takes a lot of work to keep a good marriage going—but when you start with all kinds of doubts you've got to work five times as hard to keep it going. That's what Dave and I are trying to do now. ●

Bringing Up Mother by Catherine Marshall

I find the rearing of children one of life's most turbulent and zany pursuits. Take a typical morning in our suburban household as of two years ago. Jeffrey was then 8; Chester, 11; Linda, 15; Peter John, 24. Peter had graduated from Yale, then from Princeton Seminary, and had been at home for a time awaiting a call to a church.

We were awakened on that particular morning by a commotion in the boys' bedroom. A loud yelp took me there on the run. Chester complained, "Jeff bit me." Sure enough, there were teeth marks on Chester's leg.

"You're going to be punished for this," I told Jeff sternly.

"But Chester kicked me first. Want to see where?"

I really didn't, but Jeff showed me anyway.

At that moment Linda appeared in the hallway in her night clothes, a dazed, sleepy look on her face, her feet bare. "Linda, the floor is cold. Put on your slippers."

"Can't, Mom. I put them in the washing machine and they shrank."

Obviously it was to be "one of those mornings." I went on to the kitchen to start breakfast and to fix the boys' school lunches. But it was necessary to empty Jeff's lunch box before I could fill it. I extracted two packages of bubble gum, three rocks, a pack of well-thumbed baseball cards, and a note from the teacher which he had forgotten to deliver.

The doorbell rang for a boy to hand in a Special Delivery letter. Then the telephone rang. Jeff dripped jam on his freshly pressed school pants and had to change them. Peter called out that he had a dental appointment in New York, and that he couldn't find any clean shorts. The three younger children dashed for the bus, banging the door behind them. Through the window I saw that they *had* made the bus. I turned around to pour myself a second cup of coffee, and there on the kitchen counter was Jeff's lunch which he had forgotten to take.

I sank into the nearest chair, desperately needing that cup of coffee. As I sipped it, trying to get back some calmness and perspective, in my mind I was addressing the Almighty: "Lord, what *is* this about anyway? When You put people together in families, just what *did* You really have in mind?"

Although the answer was not immediately forthcoming, it has been gradually dawning. I see now that the truth had to be doled out slowly, because had it been given to me at once, the shock would have been too great. For now I know: the family is the training ground—the testing center—where sinners get on with the painful process of being pummeled into saints. I fear that God is not half so concerned with our being what we call "happy" in this life (in His eyes, happiness never is an end in itself anyway, but a dividend) as in our being hammered and chiseled and molded into the characters He meant us to be all along.

And what is the most sure-fire method of rubbing off rough edges, forging us, shaping and molding us? Yes, parents rubbing against children; children bowing the will to parental authority as training for that bowing to God's authority so necessary for any committed life—writ small enough in the family for growing minds to grasp the lesson; children learning to get along with one another, yes, even if there is some biting and kicking on the bedroom floor in the process. For whether we like it or not, the Creator insists that we get on with being "members one of another." And if we cannot manage this in small family units, by what perverse reasoning do we imagine that we can succeed at it in the nation and across the world?

I might think the plan grossly unfair, did I not know that even Jesus Himself had to get along with other children in His home in Nazareth. It is therefore no small comfort that in this as in all things, He is a High Priest who knows what we are up against, can sympathize with our weaknesses, and has in all points been tempted as we are (Hebrews 4:15).

Nor do I have to search far to find the temptations our children hand me—such as sins of disposition. Take a command like, "Be ye angry and sin not," or like Jesus asking us to forgive 70 times seven. Jeff, age 9 now, still looks like an impish boy angel. At least that is the way other people see him. Boy angel or not, he is stubborn and recalcitrant and often deflects from authority. There is the matter of his repeatedly leaving ink cartridges in his pants pocket and so ruining an entire tub of laundry. So then each time I put away the family underwear—now looking as if it had the navy-blue measles—I get first rate practice in the art of forgiveness.

Then there is Jeff's habit of forgetting everything because his little mind is floating around somewhere on Cloud 9. So he cannot wear his PF Flyers because he left them at the public tennis courts; his sweater was abandoned at Don's house; it is impossible to do his assignment because he left his book at school. As I step on the accelerator for those time-consuming trips to the tennis courts and to Don's house to collect possessions, I must find the way "not to let the sun go down on my wrath."

And there is that passage in Holy Writ about letting "patience have her perfect work." What could be better calculated to teach patience than trying to drum manners or tidiness into children? It is the limitless nature of the task that staggers me as I ask for the 687th time, "Who left towels on the bathroom floor this time?" . . . "Boys, this room is a mess. You must hang up your clothes.". . . .

Still, my husband Len and I have had evidence in the last two years that some progress is being made. Nor is all of the stretching "unto a perfect man, unto the measure of the stature of the fulness of Christ" (Ephesians 4:13) on the side of father and mother.

Linda, 16, is away at boarding school in Troy, New York. At any given holiday she arrives on the plane from Kennedy airport, exults in the warm Florida air, "Mom, it was *ten above* in New York. . . ." As soon as she gets inside the door at home, she bearhugs the boys, croons over Bootsy, our miniature collie, and then immediately begins offering advice.

During Christmas vacation the introductory subject for the first meal was Boys' Posture At Mealtimes. . . . "Jeff, elbows off the table. . . . Shoulders back. *Back!*" Three minutes later, "Chester, will you stop slumping . . . ? No, straighter. You can't be *that* lazy." Five minutes later, "Jeff, shove your chair in closer. Maybe that will help. Why your back is positively *bowed*. Do you want to get a dowager's hump at age 9!" And so on—and on.

I sat there wondering how long the boys would take this from their sister. Finally Jeff sighed and cast his innocent blue eyes upon her, the dark eyelashes fluttering. "Linda, when are you *leaving?*"

But Linda was glad to have a lot of vacation left because she was full of reform work to be done on the rest of us too. There was the matter of Family Prayers after the evening meal. Due to many interruptions of children's activities, we had managed this only spottily. Linda now told us off. "I think that we should read the Bible every night, around the dining room table too. When we sit around the living room, the boys' attention can wander more. And before we begin to read, we should have a little prayer asking that the Spirit of God help us to understand what we read. When *I* don't do that, *I* don't get much out of Bible reading. But when I do pray that little prayer, then I get all sorts of great ideas."

Len and I were looking at her in astonishment. Could this be the same girl who spends hours curling her eyelashes, who helps keep the hair spray manufacturers in business; whose possessions are seldom organized; whose father agonizes while he helplessly watches both her and the clock as she tries to assemble possessions to catch a plane?

But this new Linda had not finished with her suggested reform for Family Prayers. "And after the Bible reading, then I think we should hold hands around the table and pray for our real problems as a family for *that* day."

In a case like that, what can parents do but come docilely to heel?

As for Peter John, my 26-year-old son, he is now the senior missionary of our children. This too is a switch, for during his Yale days he was definitely of no such mind. Then while attending a conference of the Fellowship of Christian Athletes at Estes Park, Colorado, one afternoon he handed his life over to Jesus Christ. Since then amazing changes have come for him.

Before that, Peter's stock had been low with Linda. Then her attitude toward him did a rightabout. It was Peter who was able to do for Linda what parents can seldom do for any of their children.

Please do not mistake me. This is not braggadocio about our children. There is still much territory to be won, painful step by painful step on our way toward that Celestial City. Linda has just acquired a driver's license, and we now look forward—or do we?—to that period of teenage pleas to use the family car and to dating with its attendant strains on father and mother.

So viewing the way I have traveled the last few years, I know now that if we parents want to get on with God's plan for us, only one way is open: *commitment to marriage and to parenthood as a vocation.* No ducking out, no fleeing, no excuses. I have found out the hard way that half-measures result only in pain.

On the other hand, when we come to heel the rewards are great. Such as the guarantee of no loneliness and no rigidity as one grows older. And the impossibility of concluding that the world is going to the dogs right away so long as one has an immediate stake in the next generation. Or like irrepressible boys with wings on one side and collapsible horns on the other who keep the joy of life alive. For with one up and three to go, after that come grandchildren. Peace? Sweet peace? Who wants it anyway! ●

Love, Honor, and *Obey?* by Elisabeth Elliot Leitch

The God who controls the wheeling galaxies and who spoke before the foundation of the world must be the God who holds the smallest circumstance of your life in his hands. We are encompassed on all sides by the Almighty. "His tender mercies are over all his works," "steadfast love surrounds him who trusts in the Lord," and "underneath are the everlasting arms." Over, around, underneath. We are enfolded.

Yet God does not coerce us into doing his will. He has given us free choice, and it is in this freedom that you have chosen to marry. You have answered the questions I posed for you a year ago when you were trying to define and sort out your feelings.

1. Is this the man you want to spend the rest of your life with? That's every day of every week of every month of every year from now till one of you dies.

2. Is he punctual or habitually late? Orderly or disorderly? A reader or a TV watcher? An outdoor man or an indoor man?

3. Does he like your family? Treat you as you think a woman ought to be treated? Have men friends? Have approximately the same education you have? Like the kind of food you like to cook? Come from a home similar to yours? Like your friends? Like to entertain, and would you be proud to have him as host at the other end of the table? Laugh at the same jokes you do?

4. Can you agree on sex? In-laws? Children and their training? Money? Your respective roles in the home?

You have faced all these questions and the important areas of concern that they point to. Let me assure you that I've known happy couples of which one is an indoor person and the other an outdoor one, or one punctual and the other late, but it requires particular grace, and it's just as well to consider in advance whether or not you think it's going to be worth it. Later, when you're up against it, remind yourself that it's worth it!

You know that I do not insist that every question under 3. must be answered Yes if your marriage is to be a success. And, of course, agreement in matters of 4. can only be in principle until you've had the chance to work on them as husband and wife. Deep, underlying principles will determine your handling of these things, and you must thoroughly agree on these before you agree to marry a man. This is why I did not include religion on the list. "Religion" is not simply one of many matters to be debated about on a par with child-training and the treatment of in-laws. It will determine the child-training and how you treat your in-laws. It is the foundation of your life. As soon as you begin discussing the things on the list you will be discussing religion, for "all our problems are theological ones."

Mutual commitment to a common belief is the only solid base for lasting communion, in marriage or in any other fellowship. Anything less will not stand the test of living.

Your most recent letter to me said, "Oh, Mama, it gets better and better!" You spoke of the utter peace and contentment you know when you are with him. We can believe that God has answered our prayers—mine of years' standing, "Keep her from and for the man she is to marry" ("from" meaning until his chosen time, that you would not hurry ahead of his will)—and yours to be guided to the man of his choice. And so you wear his ring.

When the wedding ring is put on your finger, you will have finally sealed your choice. It is this man, and this one alone, whom you have chosen for "as long as ye both shall live." There have been many revisions and improvisations in modern weddings; in one of them the phrase has been changed from "as long as ye both shall live" to "as long as we both shall love." This cuts the heart out of the deepest meaning of the wedding. It is a vow you are making before God and before witnesses, a vow you will by God's grace keep, which does not depend on your moods or feelings or "how things turn out." As others have said, love does not preserve the marriage; the marriage preserves love.

When you make a choice, you accept the limitations of that choice. To accept limitation requires maturity. The child has not yet learned that it can't have everything. What it sees it wants. What it does not get it screams for. It has to grow up to realize that saying Yes to happiness often means saying No to yourself.

Karl Barth, in his superb treatise on Man and Woman in *Church Dogmatics*, defines marriage as "the form of encounter of male and female in which the free, mutual, harmonious choice of love on the part of a particular man and woman leads to a responsibly undertaken life-union which is lasting, complete, and exclusive. It is the *telos*, the goal and center of the relationship between man and woman. The sphere of male and female is wider than that of marriage, embracing the whole complex of relations at the center of which marriage is possible."

What difference from the casual liaisons entered into by young couples who, in seeking to be "free," have dispensed with that responsibly undertaken life-union. Their union is not responsible to anyone; it is not lasting, complete, or exclusive, and as such cannot possibly bring them the joy they so desperately hope for. All manner of alternatives have been tried and none has produced what it promised. No marriage "experiment" has any validity, lacking the essential ingredient of total and irrevocable commitment.

But how can they know commitment to one another when they have made no higher commitment? Thank God for a loyalty not only to each other but a common higher loyalty to God. That is a sound basis for marriage.

But don't be deceived. Many couples have shared this loyalty (some I know shared almost nothing else) and have found that their marriage was far from ideal. As long as we are "in the flesh" we'll have trouble in the flesh. But God knows the purpose of heart. He sees the direction a couple has taken when they have made up their minds to seek "things which are above." There is a whole world of difference between those who look only for their own happiness in this world and those who know that their true happiness lies in the will of God.

When they encounter trouble they know where to turn, for they know that they are still under the command of God; they are not forsaken. They *know* that they are insufficient in themselves, that human love breaks down, and that there is never a point at which they can say, "We've arrived," and are no longer in need of grace.

Your love is a gift, and if it is a gift you are grateful to the Giver.

To acknowledge your gratitude to him is also to acknowledge your dependence on him, to acknowledge above all the authority of Christ. That is a good place to begin a marriage.

Marriage is a dynamic, not a static, relationship. It gets either better or worse. As people either grow or deteriorate, relationships between them must grow or deteriorate. A common explanation offered for marital incompatibility is "We outgrew each other." It's been said that if a couple doesn't grow together they grow apart. But for the couple who have in all seriousness said their vows before God and in the presence of witnesses the possibility of growing apart need not be allowed. It need never be something which "happens to" them, as though they were bystanders injured by some force which they were powerless to protect themselves from. They have willed to love and live together. They stand, not helpless, but in relation to God, each responsible to fulfill his vows to the other. Each determines to do the will of God so that together they move toward "the measure of the stature of the fullness of Christ." And, if God is viewed as the apex of a triangle of which they are the two base points, movement toward him necessarily decreases the distance between them. Drawing near to God means drawing nearer to each other, and this means growth and change.

There are tensions. The strength of a great cathedral lies in the thrust and counterthrust of its buttresses and arches. Each has its own function and each its peculiar strength. This is the way I see the dynamics of a good marriage. It is not strength pitted against weakness. It is two kinds of strength, each meant to fortify the other in special ways. It is not a weakness for a sailboat to submit itself to the rules of sailing. That submission *is* her strength. It is the rules that enable the boat to utilize her full strength, to harness the wind and thus take to herself the wind's strength. It was not weakness in the Son of God that made him obey the will of the Father. It was power—the power of his own will to will the father's will.

There is in a good marriage both dependence and independence on both sides. Your husband needs you to be different from him, to be what you are alone, to be what he can never be and what he needs and wants. Only in this way can you be what you are in relation to him. Only in this way can you complement him. He depends on you to be his complement; you depend on him to be yours. He is independent of you in his differences—you are woman, distinct, wholly other, opposite. "Nevertheless," said the Apostle Paul, "in the Lord woman is not independent of man nor man of woman; for as woman was made from man so man is now born of woman. And all things are from God." Men and women cannot and must not try to live life without reference to the opposite sex. They are interdependent and are meant to acknowledge and confront one another. It is this confrontation—most clearly realized in marriage—that makes it of enormous importance that the sexes not be confused, ignored, played down or played off against each other. We need each other. A husband and wife need to be husband and wife, not buddies. The dynamics must be maintained as the Architect intended.

Your provider may someday lose his job. Your strength may show unexpected weakness. Your knight in armor may experience a public defeat. Your teacher may make a serious mistake that you tried to warn him about. Your lover may become a helpless patient, sick, sore, and sad, needing your presence and care every minute of the day and night. "This isn't the man I married," you will say, and it will be true. But you married him for better or for worse, in sickness and in health, and those tremendous promises took into account the possibility of radical change. That was why promises were necessary.

There are things in life which can make what seems to be a mockery out of the solemn promises. "To love, honor, and obey" your husband can seem the last ironies in the face of the unspeakable humiliations and indignities of illness. Love, honor, and obey this beaten, anguished, angry man who will not take his pill? The vows are serious. Staggeringly serious. But you did not take them trusting in your own strength to perform. The grace that enabled you to take those vows will be there to draw on when the performance of them seems impossible.

Marriage is not the sole task to which any of us is called. Women who have no career as such are certainly called to a variety of tasks besides marriage. Parenthood is a task and one which, like a career, all too often eclipses the vocation of marriage so that a couple forgets that they have been called to one another and thinks only of the family. Every task requires faith.

We all would like a simple formula for sorting out the priorities, and no one is going to give us one. God alone, who calls you to your task, will help you to know where the balance lies as you weigh your responsibilities before him, and pray and trust. "The just shall live by faith" is the rule in marriage as in all other spheres of life.

Is being a woman fundamentally different from being a man? Is there anything inherent in the nature of human beings or of human society that requires certain roles or tasks to be associated with one sex or the other?

In order to learn what it means to be a woman we must start with the One who made her.

Every Sunday morning in our church we repeat a creed. You know what it says. "I believe in one God, the Father, the Almighty, Maker of all things visible and invisible." There's a statement that has nothing whatever to do with my personal opinions or emotions. It's a statement of objective fact, accepted by faith, and when I stand up in the company of other Christians and repeat this statement I am not talking about myself at all. The only thing I am saying about myself is that I submit to these truths. This is where I stand; this is Reality.

If in fact I do believe these *great* things we say and sing together, then those *little* things (and what is not little by comparison?) will be taken care of. I take my position, I get my bearings. I need to do this often—more often, it seems, in these days when so many have altogether lost their bearings.

We sometimes hear the expression "the accident of sex," as though one's being a man or a woman were a triviality. It is very far from being a triviality. It is our nature. It is the modality under which we live all our lives; it is what you and I are called to be—called by God, this God who is in charge. It is our destiny, planned, ordained, fulfilled by an all-wise, all-powerful, all-loving Lord.

God is the Almighty, the Creator, a God of order, harmony, design. We believe the creation story in the first two chapters of the Bible, and we delight in knowing that the Maker of all that list of marvels delighted when he looked at them. He made each thing according to the Word of his power, and when he looked at it he saw that it was good.

He made man in his own image, and then for the first time God saw something that was not good. It was not good for the man to be alone. God determined to make a helper fit for him, and it was after this decision, according to Genesis 2:19, that he made the animals and birds—as though from among them such a helper might be chosen.

The animals are there, fellow-creatures with us of the same Creator-God, fellow-sufferers, mute and mysterious. "But for the man there was not found a helper fit for him."

God might have given Adam another man to be his friend, to walk and talk and argue with if that was his pleasure. But Adam needed more than the companionship of the animals or the friendship of a man. He needed a helper, specially designed and specially prepared to fill that role in his life. It was a woman God gave him, a woman, "meet," fit, suitable, entirely appropriate for him, made of his very bones and flesh.

You can't make proper use of a thing unless you know what it was made for, whether it is a safety pin or a sailboat. To me it is a wonderful thing to be a woman under God—to know, first of all that we were *made* ("So God created man in his own image, in the image of God he created him; male and female he created them.") and then that we were made *for* something ("The rib which the Lord God had taken from the man he made into a woman and brought her to the man.").

This was the original idea. This is what woman was for. The New Testament refers back clearly and strongly to this purpose: "For man was not made for woman, but woman for man. Neither was man created for woman, but woman for man." Some texts are susceptible of differing interpretations, but for the life of me I can't see any ambiguities in this one.

All creatures, with two exceptions that we know of, have willingly taken the places appointed to them. The Bible speaks of angels who rebelled and therefore were cast down out of heaven, and of the fall of man. Adam and Eve were not satisfied with the place assigned. They refused the single limitation set them in the Garden of Eden and thus brought sin and death to the whole world. It was, in fact, the woman, Eve, who saw the opportunity to be something other than she was meant to be—the Serpent convinced her that she could easily be "like God"—and she took the initiative.

We have no way of knowing whether a consultation with her husband first might have led to an entirely different conclusion. Perhaps it might. Perhaps if she had put the question to him and he had had to ponder the matter he would have seen the deadly implications, and have refused the fruit. But Eve had already tried it. She had not been struck dead; she offered it to her husband. How could he refuse? Eve was undoubtedly a beautiful woman. She was the woman God had given him. She was only testing out what seemed an unnecessary and trivial restriction, and her boldness had been rewarded. She had gotten away with it, and now why shouldn't Adam do the same?

What sort of world might it have been if Eve had refused the Serpent's offer and had said to him instead, "Let me not be like God. Let me be what I was made to be—let me be a woman"?

But the sin was fatal beyond their worst imaginings. It was *hubris*, a lifting up of the soul in defiance of God, the pride that usurps another's place. It is a damnable kind of pride.

But there is another kind of pride, one which every man and woman under God ought to cultivate. Isak Dinesen defines it in her beautiful book *Out of Africa*:

"Pride is faith in the idea that God had, when he made us. A proud man is conscious of the idea, and aspires to realize it. He does not strive toward a happiness, or comfort, which may be irrelevant to God's idea of him. His success is the idea of God, successfully carried through, and he is in love with his destiny."

The universe moves at the command of God, and men and women are at all times under that command, but, distinct from robins and lobsters, they have been given the power to disobey. They are capable of doing a great many things they are not supposed to do. The ability to do them is not a command to do them. It is not even permission. This simple fact, so obvious in the physical realm (we know perfectly well we're not supposed to smash other people in the face, capable and eager to do so though we may sometimes be), is easily obscured in the intellectual and spiritual realms.

We discern in ourselves certain propensities or even gifts and, without thought for possible restrictions which may be placed upon their use, start wielding them. The results may be far more destructive than smashing somebody in the face. Men and women who have used their minds, their talents, and their genius to move multitudes to evil have used the minds, talents, and genius given to them by their Creator. But they have not asked what God has commanded. They have not offered themselves first to him, trusting his direction for their proper sphere of operation.

We are called to be women. The fact that I am a woman does not make me a different kind of Christian, but the fact that I am a Christian does make me a different kind of woman. For I have accepted God's idea of me, and my whole life is an offering back to him of all that I am and all that he wants me to be.

For the Christian woman, whether she is married or single, there is the call to serve. A news magazine recently reported an adult course offered in "Assertive Behavior," which, according to the descriptions of sample situations, amounted to a course in boorishness. One lesson, for example, encouraged women to break free from the "compassion trap." In response to this article a reader wrote, "I cannot understand why a woman would object to being a part of the 'compassion trap'—the need to serve others and provide tenderness and compassion at all times. What this society needs is more emphasis on the need to serve others, and provide tenderness, compassion, cooperation and love."

Do the women's liberationists want to be liberated from being women? No, they would say, they want to be liberated from society's stereotypes of what women are supposed to be. There are, according to their theorists, no fundamental differences between men and women. It is all a matter of conditioning. Some very interesting facts have been uncovered by scientists which feminists will have to treat very gingerly, for they show that it is not merely society which determines how the sexes will behave. There are strong biological reasons (a matter of hormones) why the male has always dominated and will continue to dominate in every society.

The idea of matriarchy is mythical, I've learned, for not one that can be documented has ever existed. Doesn't it seem strange that male dominance has been universal if it's purely social conditioning? One would expect to see at least a few examples of societies where women rather than men held the positions of highest status. (The existence of reigning queens proves nothing, since they have their position by heritage, not by achievement, choice, or election.) Isn't it really much easier to believe that the feelings of men and women throughout history bear a direct relationship to some innate prerequisite?

It was God who made us different, and he did it on purpose. Recent scientific research is illuminating, and as has happened before, corroborates ancient truth which mankind has always recognized. God created male and female, the male to call forth, to lead, initiate and rule, and the female to respond, follow, adapt, submit. Even if we held to a different theory of origin, the physical structure of the female would tell us that woman was made to receive, to bear, to be acted upon, to complement, to nourish.

The notion of hierarchy comes from the Bible. The words "superior" and "inferior" refer originally to position, not to intrinsic worth. A person sitting in the top of a stadium would be superior to—higher up than—a person on the front row. Cherubim and seraphim were superior to archangels, archangels to angels, and man was "made a little lower than the angels." The earth and its creatures were formed prior to man, so man's position in God's scale is not necessarily determined by the chronology of creation, for that would give the animals a superior place. His position was assigned to him when he was commanded to subdue the earth and have dominion over the fish of the sea and over the birds of the air and over every living thing that moves upon the earth.

Acceptance of the divinely ordered hierarchy means acceptance of authority—first of all, God's authority, and then those lesser authorities which he has ordained. A husband and wife are both under God, but their positions are not the same. A wife is to submit herself to her husband. The husband's "rank" is given to him by God, as the angels' and animals' ranks are assigned, not chosen or earned. The mature man acknowledges that he did not earn or deserve his place by superior intelligence, virtue, strength, or amiability. The mature woman acknowledges that submission is the will of God for her, and obedience to this will is no more a sign of weakness in her than it was in the Son of Man when he said, "Lo, I come—to do thy will, O God."

Common sense has told women in all societies in all ages that the care of the home was up to them. Men have been providers. There are surely circumstances in our complex modern society which call for modifications. If we have become so mature and open-minded and adaptable and liberated that the commands of Scripture directed to wives—"adapt," "submit," "subject"—lose their meaning, if the word "head" no longer carries any connotation of authority, and hierarchy has come to mean tyranny, we have been drowned in the flood of liberation ideology.

God wants us to be whole and secure and strong, and one of the ways to find that wholeness and security and strength is to submit ourselves to the authorities he has put over us.

Submission for the Lord's sake does not amount to servility. It does not lead to self-destruction, the stifling of gifts, personhood, intelligence, and spirit. If obedience itself requires a suicide of the personality (as one writer claims) we would have to conclude that obedience to Christ demands this. But the promises he's given us hardly point to self-destruction: "I will give you rest." "My peace I give unto you." "I am come that they might have life, and that they might have it more abundantly." "Whosoever believeth in me shall have everlasting life." "Whoso drinketh of the water that I shall give him shall never thirst." "Whoever loses his life for my sake will preserve it." "It is your Father's good pleasure to give you the kingdom."

God is not asking anybody to become a zero. What was the design of the Creator in everything that he made? He wanted it to be good, that is, perfect, precisely what he meant, free in its being the thing he intended it to be. When he commanded Adam to "subdue" and "have dominion over" the earth he was not commanding him to destroy its meaning or existence. He was, we may say, "orchestrating," giving the lead to one, subduing another, to produce a full harmony for his glory.

When Paul speaks of the subordination of women he bases his argument on the creative order. The woman was created from and for the man. It follows naturally that she had to be created after the man. Woman's secondary chronological position does not prove an inferior intelligence. But those who rule out the possibility of sexual differences in intellectual gifts are not taking all the data into account.

In a book called *The Inevitability of Patriarchy*, Steven Goldberg goes to infinite pains to show that he is in no way suggesting that men are generally superior to women. They are *different*, and their differences are hormonally determined. For the Christian who believes that the traditional patriarchal order is not merely cultural and sociological but has its foundation in theology, it is interesting to discover that it has also a valid biological foundation.

There is a spiritual principle involved here. It is the will of God. From Genesis to Revelation we are shown in countless stories of God's dealings with people that it is his will to make them free, to give them joy. Sometimes the process of freeing them is a painful one. It meant death for the Son of Man—his life for ours. He came not to condemn, not to imprison, not to enslave. He came to give life.

And it is the will of God that woman be subordinate to man in marriage. Marriage is used in the Old Testament to express the relation between God and his covenant people and in the New Testament between Christ and the church. No effort to keep up with the times, to conform to modern social movements or personality cults authorizes us to invert this order. Tremendous heavenly truths are set forth in a wife's subjection to her husband, and the use of this metaphor in the Bible cannot be accidental. ●

Is There Love After Marriage? by John M. Drescher

I was invited for a meal in the home of a former classmate in college. The children are in their late teens and early twenties. Their only daughter was present along with her fianceé. I observed that while we were eating this young couple would occasionally join hands. When one of them spoke, they looked into each other's eyes, and several times reached out to touch the other's arm when making a smiling response to something said. When they moved from the table to the kitchen to wash the dishes together, they shared a kiss and smiled happily at each other. They talked and laughed all the while they washed and dried dishes. They were living for each other.

Few marriages would dry up and die if half of the sentiment expressed during courtship continued after marriage. Most marriages would not only survive but would sparkle with satisfaction if partners continued the common courtesies practiced before marriage.

The dry-rot of marriage sets in because married couples in our society assume too much. We assume love will grow without nurture and cultivation. Because we take the other person for granted, we neglect words of appreciation. We assume the other will continue to be attracted to us regardless of how we appear. We assume the other person knows what we are thinking and how we feel without communicating our thoughts and feelings.

Maintaining a marriage is like maintaining a house: good marriages are always the result of constant care and continual repair. Like a house, if we let small repair work go, eventually major problems result. Ignore a small leak and sooner or later the living room will be flooded. Neglect the little termites and the foundation will

finally fall. Put off painting and the appearance will become dark and forbidding.

What specifically is necessary for the maintenance of a good and happy marriage?

First, if marriage is to have meaning, time is involved, no less than in any other important enterprise. Before marriage, a couple takes steps to spend time together, to go places together, and to talk together. Too often, after marriage each partner goes a separate way. Without meaningful moments together each day, a dullness will creep into our love and we become strangers to each other while living under the same roof.

Second, to avoid the dry-rot we must habitually practice the common courtesies of life. If such things as consideration, kindness, and words and acts of love were necessary for the cultivation of love in courtship, these graces are just as necessary for the maintaining and maturing of love in marriage. Strange as it seems, the very things which built our love in courtship are the things we often let slip so soon afterward.

The neglect of loving words and tones of voice to each other in marriage would not be tolerated during the dating period. Few if any marriages would develop dry-rot if husbands and wives were even as gracious to each other as they are to strangers and friends.

This means the same little phrases of love in courtship such as "I love you," "May I help you?" "I'm sorry" and "Forgive me" must be continued for a happy marriage. This means that little gifts selected with care, love letters when away, good-bye and welcome home kisses, remembrances on special occasions, the loving touch of the hand and all other expressions of love which we practiced so eagerly during courtship must be maintained for love to continue.

Love is a tender plant. Without constant care and nurture it dries up and dies. And no marriage can have vitality and bliss if these small courtesies are absent.

To prevent the dry-rot we must continue our efforts to be attractive to each other. Before marriage all efforts were made to appear our very best. We seek to have a spirit of happiness and helpfulness when we are with each other. We seek to be attractive physically and intellectually. Often, however, married partners slip into a pattern of life which is almost opposite. Careless dress and physical appearance is too much assumed. Overweight and outright neglect of personal hygiene take over. Rather than a joyful, happy attitude, a spirit of gloom and drudgery settles in.

Another way to prevent the dry-rot in marriage is to keep talking. When a marriage goes stale, one of the sure marks is that we have stopped talking. That is, we have stopped talking about those things which really matter to us, how we feel, and about our desires for each other and ourselves.

In courtship we learn to know and understand each other by talking. We can't talk enough. Now in marriage the main problem is the inability to talk. Communication becomes rusty.

Nothing else will substitute for conversation. For love to continue to grow, we must be willing to share ourselves. A test of love and the way to grow in oneness is to share deeply and discuss openly with acceptance and appreciation all that concerns us. Self-disclosure, self-awareness, non-possessive caring, risk-taking, trust, acceptance, and feedback are involved when there is good communication.

Married love cannot survive the silent treatment any more than courtship can. So to avoid the dry-rot, keep talking about what matters. Use "feel words" such as "I like" or "I don't like" and "I'm angry when" which do not insult the other and which encourage a response. Learn to listen to each other until you have heard what the other is saying and feeling. Marriage is a life duet, not prima donna solos. ●